Hosea Commentary

Return to the Lord

Martin Murphy

Second Edition

Hosea Commentary:
Return to the Lord

Published by: Theocentric Publishing
             1069A Main Street
             Chipley, Florida 32428

             www.theocentricpublishing.com

ISBN 9780998560601

To Dr. Richard Pratt for teaching me the principles of
Old Testament interpretation

Preface

This brief commentary and exposition of Hosea comes from my preparation to preach and teach through this book. The notes are conceptual. They are not intended to be a thorough analytical commentary, but rather I tried to summarize the larger body of doctrine into short brief statements. These brief notes will be useful to pastors, Sunday School teachers, and laymen who want to dig deeper into the Word of God.

Return to the Lord is more than a title; it describes the spiritual condition of Israel and may be applied to the people of God in every generation. Hosea understood that the Israelites were religious, but in their religious zeal they accumulated a host of false gods to worship. The sin nature will always try to deceive people to wander away from God. Hosea's message will challenge Christians to return to the Lord.

The format is not typical because these notes will require additional study from Scripture and dependable commentaries. The line spacing gives the reader an opportunity to meditate on the concepts and make additional notes.

References to Hosea that are in **bold** ought to be read and kept in the context of the current exposition. Other Scripture references are in brackets. They should be read and considered in the context that I placed them.

Table of Contents

Religion in Reverse

Hosea 1:1-11; 2:1

The Lord gives His people a message through the prophet Hosea. It is their duty to listen to the Lord.

Before we go any further in Hosea let me remind you of the Lord's words at the end of this book:

> ➢ Who is wise?
> ➢ Let him understand these things
> ➢ Who is prudent?
> ➢ Let Him know them
> ➢ For the ways of the Lord are right
> ➢ The righteous walk in them
> ➢ But transgressors stumble in them.
> (Hosea 14:9)

This is a book about religion because we find religious words dominate Hosea's preaching. Those words are wisdom, understanding, prudence, and knowledge. Every prominent religion known throughout human history has used those words to make a place in history. Christians are not looking for place; they are looking for a person! That person is the one true and living God. God's children live according to wisdom, prudence, understanding, and knowledge. The unrighteous despise wisdom, prudence, understanding, and knowledge.

A few introductory remarks about the book of Hosea will be necessary to understand the message. The larger context of this prophecy begins by God making a covenant with Israel at Mt. Sinai, but Israel loved the ways of the surrounding nations more than she loved God. Out of His grace, God still gave His people a home and eventually established a permanent place of worship in Jerusalem.

God's people in the Old Testament are often referred to as the nation of Israel. For the purpose of understanding this Old Testament prophecy in the contemporary church, I will call God's people in the Old Testament, the Old Testament church or simply the church underage. The New Testament church is a congregation of God's people and likewise Old Testament Israel is a congregation of God's people. God's people are always God's people whether in the Old Testament or the New Testament. The term *Old Testament church* or the *church underage* serves as a reminder to apply this prophecy to the contemporary church.

The Old Testament church underage divided after the death of Solomon. Ten of the twelve tribes of Israel became the northern kingdom and two of the tribes became the southern kingdom. It was like a New Testament church split.

Hosea's prophecy took place over a period of about forty years, from about 760 B.C. to 720 B.C. One of the most significant historical events in Judeo-Christian history occurred in 722 B.C. with the fall and dispersion of the northern kingdom.

God designated the Temple in Jerusalem as the place for the congregation to meet for worship. The northern kingdom disobeyed the Lord by forsaking temple worship at the place commanded by God. It was religion in reverse for the ten tribes of the northern kingdom for about two hundred years.

Similarly is the analogy of the Christian religion in North America. The New England Puritans wanted to obey God's mandate in Scripture for worship. They only survived a few generations. I believe the death of Jonathan Edwards was the end of Puritanism and the beginning of the decline of the evangelical church in North America. It was not long until churches began to denominate exponentially in this country and like Israel it was religion in reverse.

Hosea's prophecy occurred during a critical time for the northern kingdom and the southern kingdom. Although Hosea was probably a native of the northern kingdom, his prophecy was also important to the southern kingdom. Since Hosea lived to see the decline of godly worship and probably the destruction of the northern kingdom, this prophecy would warn the southern kingdom of God's justice. It would warn them to return to the Lord.

Hosea is too often misinterpreted because of the romantical and mystical mindset of the contemporary interpreter. Hosea speaks sometimes in symbolical and figurative language and at other times literal language with spiritual passion. Wise discernment and the use of orthodox interpretative theory are necessary to understand the message of Hosea.

Hosea acting as God's mouthpiece confronted the church underage. The contemporary church must realize the sin, which prevails in it and the possibility of judgment coming upon it.

God also gave Hosea a message of hope and restoration for the Old Testament church. The New Testament church not only has hope of restoration, but it has the promise of restoration in the New Heavens and the New Earth.

The church today, like the pilgrims in the Old Testament, are heirs of the city, which has foundations, whose builder and maker is God. Christians must never put down the trowel as they look for the celestial city. They must find their place on the wall and work to restore a broken church.

Sometimes a sermon will have two or three points or more. Hosea's message over a forty year period has two points. The first point is about the failure of Old Testament Israel, the church underage, to keep covenant with God. The second point is the hope of reformation and restoration for God's people.

As in all of Scripture, judgment was overwhelmingly

the message of this prophet and by necessity precedes reformation, restoration, and revival. Unfortunately many preachers and teachers tend to avoid language that reminds God's children of God's judgment for breaking covenant with Him. It is unfortunate because the time will come when God will judge the world with His righteous judgment. To avoid teaching such an important part of Holy Scripture is unfair to the people of God.

The literary structure of Hosea is primarily symbolic experiences that reveal God's displeasure with His people. Hosea's message of salvation is found in his prophetic announcements and metaphorical language.

The symbolic events in the first chapter of Hosea represent the religious reversal in the life of the Old Testament church. The text begins with a strange command from the Lord.

Hosea 1:2

This text is Hosea's first marriage, which primarily refers to his symbolic experience.

Hosea's marriage to Gomer is symbolic of God's experience with Israel. Hosea was obedient and married Gomer. This act represented Israel's spiritual adultery against God.

Obviously Hosea used this powerful illustration of an unhappy marriage relationship to show the Old Testament church the same sin we face today. It reveals how much the Old Testament church had reversed its attitude toward God. Then, as today, the focus was on the individual desires of the sinful heart so easily persuaded by the lies of Satan. The centrality of God and His kingdom ought to control the life and worship of Christians.

Hosea was commanded to take a wife of harlotry. The harlot was a woman living an immoral life. Harlotry is a word that relates to adultery and more specifically prostitution. The harlot in a physical sense refers to adultery in an illicit sense. Then there is spiritual adultery, which refers to the people of God seeking after other lovers to worship. Jeremiah talked about Israel backsliding by playing the harlot. Spiritual adultery is the wicked sin of idolatry.

The Old Testament church underage sought after and worshipped the same idols as the surrounding pagan nations. The church played the harlot.

The modern church has also committed spiritual adultery. She has departed from the Lord by mixing pop psychology with God's Word or following the ways of modern management to achieve success. She ought to remain true to the Word of God. The church is not the melting pot for the truth of God and lies of Satan. Religious syncretism is the mixing of the true and false together. It is always dangerous.

Spiritual adultery is much worse that physical adultery, although both are detestable in the sight of God.

Today the church lusts after the things that satisfy her desires. Spiritual adultery is not merely an indication of Old Testament immorality.

This text not only refers to a wife of harlotries, but it speaks of children of harlotries. This must refer to the immoral acts of the children. Hosea must mean that the children will be like their mother. Parents will have a profound effect on their children's lives. It is a lesson that parents learn too late in life.

The three children born to this union of Hosea with Gomer were given names by God Himself, which are symbolically significant. There is a sense in which these names reflected God's own personal relationship with the Old Testament Church.

The symbolic names represented certain characteristics found in the Old Testament church. They are particularly important when we see religion in reverse in the New Testament Church. The contemporary church ought to learn from them.

The first child was named *Jezreel*.
Hosea 1: 4-5

Jezreel is the place where Jehu massacred the House of Ahab, at the command of the Lord no less, but afterwards Jehu became wicked and worshipped the pagan idols (2 Kings 9-10).

God said he would avenge the bloodshed of *Jezreel*. The Hebrew word used to describe this is also used throughout the Old Testament as a redemptive act.

What Jehu did was wrong, but God never neglects the wrongs that are done to his people. God's hand of justice may wait a lifetime or several generations, but God will vindicate His righteousness. At the same time God will pour out His wrath on evil workers and the unjust.

Why did God avenge the blood of *Jezreel* upon the House of Jehu? Because, Jehu looked to his own ends, rather than God. Jehu was God's man at first, but his religious zeal and leadership fizzled out. The temptations he faced as king and in his society were more than he could handle.

Jehu wanted the same thing Eve was tempted with in the garden. In philosophy it refers to individualism because "I" am more important than anyone else. In politics it is known as democracy because "I" want to be in control. The centrality of the sin nature is "I am" and "I want."

Jehu was worse than Ahab. It is possible to do that which God commands, and yet really not obey God.

If God calls you into the gospel ministry, you might obey half-heartedly. You may be in the ministry, yet not exercise all the gifts God has given you thereby not really obeying the Lord.

God is the source of all power.
Hosea 1:5

The bow was a symbol of power when it was used as the primary instrument of warfare. A broken bow symbolized a loss of power. Israel's broken bow means she would experience defeat by the enemy. Without the power of the Holy Spirit the church will find defeat rather than victory.

When a particular church turns her back on sound biblical doctrine, she becomes subject to all sorts of false doctrine, because her bow is broken.

False doctrine will lead to false worship and false worship is nothing but religion in reverse.

The second child was named *Lo-Ruhamah*.
Hosea 1:6-7

The word *Lo-Ruhamah* literally translated from the Hebrew text means *not loved*. "I will not continue to show love to the House of Israel" says the Lord but "I will continue to show love to Judah."

To keep this in context Israel refers to the northern kingdom and Judah is a reference to the southern kingdom. They both make up the Old Testament Church underage. It was like having two denominations that use the same Bible, but believe opposite and different doctrine in worship and practice.

First God said *Jezreel* meaning punishment is forthcoming. Now God says *Lo Ruhamah* which means I will remove my favor and more specifically my love. Religious worship and life was in reverse in the Old Testament church because they were turning away from God.

The third child was named *Lo-Ammi*.
Hosea 1:8

The failure of God's people to keep His covenant will bring God's judgment on the entire congregation. God will not only discipline them and not love them, but here He speaks of disowning them.

This prophecy probably refers to the defeat and captivity of Samaria, the central city of the Northern kingdom, by the Assyrian King Shalmaneser V and the scattering of the Israelites among the peoples of the earth at 722 B.C.

The dispersion of God's people does not mean the Old Testament church ended, but it did mean that the greater portion of the church had turned away from God. Like Ahaz, that portion of the Old Testament church had become apostate.

The sinful heart turns away from the Lord, but the Lord never leaves His children. The apostle John gives a clear explanation about this doctrine. "They went out from us, but they were not of us; for it they had been of us, they would have continued with us" (1 John 2:19).

Religion in Reverse

Is Hosea all gloom and doom? No, absolutely not!

As always God will leave His church with a word of hope.
Hosea 1:10 - 2:1

The announcement of salvation is found in connection with God's promise to multiply His people like the sand of the sea.

God's people will be reunited under one leader, the Lord Jesus Christ. The Lord will lead His people out of this land and this present suffering into the New Heavens and the New Earth.

You can expect a reversal in religion in a true and right sense when the Lord intervenes to save His people.

- ➢ *Jezreel* will not be a sign of judgment, but a sign of salvation.

- ➢ *Lo-Ammi* (not my people) will become *Ammi* (sons of the living God).

- ➢ *Lo-Ruhamah* (not loved) will become *Ruhamah* (my loved ones).

The prophet spoke a twofold prophecy to the northern kingdom.

> ➢ A prophecy of God's curse for not keeping the Law.

> ➢ A prophecy of God's blessing because of his love and mercy for His people.

After Hosea spoke these words they were written so Judah, the southern kingdom, would not make the same fatal mistake of the northern kingdom. Judah must learn of the certainty and severity of God's judgment.

What does all this mean to us today? It means the church also faces the possibility of judgment because she has turned her back on the Word of God.

Where does that leave us as individual Christians?

> ➢ Avoid those practices that bring judgment.
> ➢ Trust Christ and Christ alone for salvation by grace through faith.
> ➢ Never lose hope in the Kingdom of Jesus Christ.

The Powerful Hand of God

Hosea 2:2-13

The text of Hosea's prophecy is unique in many ways. I use the time-tested grammatico-historical method for interpreting Scripture. If the text is obviously symbolical and figurative interpret it that way. However it is an interpretative sin to try to make the text say something it does not say.

In this context the words given to Hosea by inspiration of the Holy Spirit are symbolical and figurative. This symbolical or figurative language is variable. It is the kind of language a farmer or a religious person would understand. Strange as it may sound a judge or attorney would understand the language because it is primarily judicial. The Old Testament prophets often portrayed God as a prosecutor undertaking a court case against the law breaking people who were supposed to obey God.

Hosea's preaching was the kind of message that would have been very familiar to people who heard his voice in the northern kingdom. However when his words were put on paper, the people of the southern kingdom reading his words would also understand them. Since it is the Word of God is has application for the New Testament church.

The message from Hosea to the Old Testament church reminded the people of their failure to keep covenant with God. God speaks to His people by using the symbolical experiences of Hosea. The symbolism in chapter one is easy for anyone to understand. God commanded Hosea to marry Gomer. Hosea represents God in this symbolical experience and Gomer represents Israel.

Hosea's prophecy consists of warnings from God about the unfaithfulness of the Old Testament church. This prophecy is a record of God's announcements of judgment against the Old Testament church that has application to the New Testament church.

Along with the announcements of punishment, God also promises to restore the church. The development of events describes the powerful hand of God on His church.

God does not take pleasure in the death of a sinner. However, God will discipline His children to bring them to repentance.

Christians ought to pray for the grace of repentance. God takes pleasure in humility and faithfulness. That is the reason God will humble the individual sinner and the church collectively. It may be in the form of discipline and God may continue His chastisement in order that He might bring the individual sinner and the whole church to a consciousness of their sin.

God will then grace them with the ability to repent so

He might show mercy and compassion for His glory.

The symbolism in this text is that of a marriage of God to the Old Testament church according to His covenant of Grace. But the church turned away from her faithful husband. This action of the church is called spiritual adultery, because the church lusted after other gods.

This is all about covenant making and covenant breaking. God made a covenant with His people, just like husbands and wives make covenants with each other at a marriage ceremony. Unfortunately many couples marry without making covenants and many more break the covenants after they make them.

The husband's covenant was: "Do you promise in the presence of God to be to your wife a faithful, loving, and devoted husband, so long as you both shall live?"

The wife's covenant was: "Do you promise in the presence of God to be to your husband a faithful, loving, and obedient wife, so long as you both shall live?"

A covenant is binding. Although people break covenants every day, there will ultimately be consequences. It is always dangerous to break God's covenant.

God, as the husband, made a covenant with his church, which is His bride. God established the covenant relationship with His people. It was their responsibility to keep His covenant. "The Lord our God, the Lord is one! You shall love the Lord your God with all your heart, with all your soul, and with all your strength" (Deuteronomy 6:4-6).

What had happened is that God's bride, the Old Testament church, had become lovers of many gods by the time Hosea was called to speak to the people. They failed to love the Lord their God with all their heart, soul, and strength.

A careful study of the Bible, a careful study of the soul, and the discriminating evidence from experience reveals that too often Christians love themselves, literally idolizing themselves and show little regard for loving God.

Too often Christians love politics more than they love God. I'm not talking about national politics. I'm talking about politics in the church. How many times do Christians try to manipulate the pastor, elders, or deacons? I've actually had church leaders tell me not to preach on a certain subject because it might offend someone.

A covenant relationship with God means that the person will love God and His Word more than their own opinion. A covenant relationship with God is based on an objective standard, which is called the Word of God. Personal opinion relative to spiritual life may lead someone to worship false gods rather than the true and living God. Without God's truth sinners may love their own sin more than they love God.

When a Christian or the church entertains unbiblical doctrine and practice, it leads to false worship. The objects of false worship are false gods, therefore disregarding the true and living God. It is called spiritual adultery, because they lust after other gods.

Biblical history reveals that God's punishment for spiritual adultery has been and remains much more severe than for physical adultery.

God loves His bride, the church, and in order to save her He must discipline her for her unfaithfulness and punish her for her apostasy.

The powerful hand of God was on the church in the Old Testament and His powerful hand is still on the church today.

Hosea uses judicial language in his message because God is the judge, prosecutor, and enforcer. Israel is the defendant.
Hosea 2:2

The court scene is that of the husband and father (Hosea symbolizing God) asking His children to accuse their mother (Gomer symbolizing the church) in His own lawsuit against her. 'Bring charges' is what happens when one person sues another person.

He said, "she is not My wife nor am I her Husband." The language is more of a trial for adultery than divorce, but later it will become obvious that a symbolic divine divorce is a form of punishment to unfaithful Israel.

You might ask the question: how was the church unfaithful or why was the powerful hand of God on the church? The powerful hand of God is on the church because of her infidelity. The accusation of infidelity was easy enough to prove.
Hosea 2:4

It is amazing how worldly the church can act and then swell with conceit in her pleasures and ideas. It is so easy to develop programs that become objects of worship. It is easier to become proud of the real estate, rather than the spiritual estate. If worship turns into glorifying human accomplishments with pomp, grand rituals and performance, God may place His powerful hand on the church.

God said He would "set her like dry land." The dry land refers to waste land that has no worth of value.
Hosea 2:3

She turns away from the Word of God and hangs on to the false worship and the idolatry that goes with it. Not just idolatry, but a passionate love of idols. Then to make it double idolatry, the church turns its back on sound biblical doctrine.

It is infidelity for a professing Christian to depart from the ways of the Lord and follow the ways of men. So what happens when God's people depart from Him?

They worship false gods. They try to find contentment within themselves only to find misery and despair.

The spiritual lawsuit has been filed, the charge has been made, and the accusation of infidelity stands uncontested. The judgment follows. The powerful hand of God is upon His people when He judges them with a righteous judgment.
Hosea 2:6

The punishment described in verse six is like that of a dumb animal that tends to wander off from his owner. The Lord restrains them from the evil way by putting up a hedge with thorns. This literally refers to a fence.

If the fence does not keep them within the fold, then some kind of affliction may be needed to save them from wandering away from God. For instance, a disease may save a child of God from apostasy. Be thankful for thorns.

The language of this text warns the people of the approaching captivity and exile of God's people. God's church today may experience the heavy hand of God. God's people are sojourners in this world and even though God may chastise them, the goal is to reach the Promised Land. God disciplines His children so they will return to Him.

Another reason the powerful hand of God is on the church is because of her ingratitude.
Hosea 2:8

This verse describes a church that is not grateful for the blessings of God. Why? Although more will be said about this later in his prophecy, it is because of ignorance. The Bible says, "she did not know." It is the same world view commonly known as agnosticism. It simply means "I don't know." In many cases "and I don't care" may be added.

The unfaithful wife is foolish, thoughtless and forgetful. God gave Israel a great harvest of the most valuable crops. The gold and silver flowed because of excellent trade conditions and a good economy. The Old Testament church failed to realize that it was God who gave all these things. Rather than praising God, they gave the credit to Baal, the false god of their worship.

So what happens when God's people forget and ignore His great blessings? The powerful hand of God is upon His people when He judges them.
Hosea 2:9-13

God will publicly embarrass the church so that she will turn back to Him. All the joy of her worship services will turn into scandal and be subject to ridicule by the unbelieving world. God's judgment was and still is loving, compassionate and merciful to a wicked and rebellious people.

The church collectively tends to misuse and abuse the gifts God has given to the church. She turns her back on God. She looks for success rather than faithfulness and justice. She tends to trust in the abundance of her material wealth rather than God. She leads her flock to believe that career becomes more important than godliness.

God's response should open the eyes of the rebellious child.

God's punishment includes taking away food, drink, and clothes. For some people those are luxuries; for other people they are necessities.

God will stop true religious worship to prevent false worship.

The big question: what must God's people do?

The big answer: return to God!

"If you will return, O Israel, says the Lord, Return to Me" (Jeremiah 4:1).

Return to His Word.

Return to true worship according to the Word of God.

Submissively, humbly and genuinely return to God.

An Engagement Forever

Hosea 2:14-23

The first three chapters of Hosea are symbolical experiences of the prophet Hosea and a woman named Gomer. God instructed Hosea to take a wife of harlotry and her name was Gomer. She had three children by Hosea, but she was an unfaithful wife.

Hosea went to court, brought charges against her because she committed adultery. The symbolism in this text implies a divorce, but he never stopped loving her. God uses these symbolical experiences of Hosea to remind the church of her relationship with God.

In the first three chapters, Hosea represents God in these symbolical experiences and Gomer represents the bride of Christ called Israel in the Old Testament and the church in the New Testament.

This is a remarkable text as it shows the intensity of God's emotions controlled by His absolute holiness and justice.

Too often God is thought of as cold, distant, and unconcerned about the struggles Christians face in this life. Too often God is portrayed as the Almighty who waits to terrorize people when they commit crimes against Him.

This text disproves such ideas. As a judge God punishes those whom He loves and as a husband He embraces them tenderly so they will have hope for the future.

The picture in the first half of chapter two is that of God's heavy hand of judgment on His church. The powerful hand of God's judgment was a result of the infidelity and ingratitude of His bride, the church.

It seems the Old Testament church forgot how God delivered Israel out of Egypt into the wilderness. It was to humble them and show them that God's hand in providence is always good for His people. There may be times when God's providence appears to be bad, but actually it is good.

The symbolical divorce was not for the purpose of escaping a bad marriage, but a punishment to awaken the Old Testament church to her senses. The application must be applied to the New Testament church.

The relationship between God and His bride (the church) had been severed because she went after other lovers. She loved the false gospel because it sounded so good. The false gospel is salvation by works. The false gospel will boost the ego and compliment the feeling of self-salvation. Contrary to the false gospel, the true gospel is salvation by grace.

The church loves the false gods of this world, because they are supposed to bring happiness. The church loves managerial theory and replaces the Word of God with psychological therapy. Some of the most popular false gods are the productions that come from the aesthetic realm.

The church is inclined to love herself and wants to be satisfied according to her own desires.

The true gospel is not popular at all. The church forgets that God's law must precede the true gospel so that the sinner will be aware of his or her sin. If people are unable see their guilt and sins, they will not be able to repent. If they are unable to repent there is no evidence of salvation.

If you think you have done anything to deserve a right relationship with God, you are not able to receive the righteousness of Christ. When Christians find themselves in the wilderness of this world, they realize the only way out is by the grace of God.

If the church in the wilderness looks at the ways of the world and adopts them, she will believe and live according to the system of the world. The system of the world makes false promises by false gods that produce false joy.

Do you know what Christians want today? Too often their only concern is happiness! They could care less about goodness. They could care less about truth!

They just want to feel happy and successful, so the sermon title may be:

➢ Three Steps to Successful Marriage.

> ➤ Four Steps to Financial Independence.
> ➤ Five Steps to a Fruitful Quiet Time.
> ➤ Six Steps to the Altar.
> ➤ Seven Steps to Heaven.

The sermon that is never preached, that should be, is "One Step to Hell."

All the gimmicks in the world will not bring God's saving grace or God's salvation to the soul of the sinner.

Do you know what will save a sinner and ultimately the church collectively? I'll tell you! God in His mercy and compassion will save the true church by grace. If God disciplines His church, it is because of her sins. His discipline is for the purpose of reconciliation and restoration. The text in Hosea is about restoration, symbolized by an engagement forever.

The symbolic divine divorce represented by the exile precedes an eternal betrothal. The exile of the northern kingdom in 722 B.C. and the exile of the southern kingdom in 586 B.C. are not merely historical facts. The spiritual decline in the church provoked God's wrath. I call it religion in reverse because it is turning away from the true and living God.

Hosea preaches to the heart of the matter.
Hosea 2:19-20

Christians today may not be familiar with the betrothal process because it has never been widely practiced in the American culture. It was a common practice in the

Old Testament as it still is in many cultures in the world. The betrothal is a legally binding promise of marriage.

The Bible explains the betrothal. "If a young woman who is a virgin is betrothed to a husband, and a man finds her in the city and lies with her, then you shall bring them both out to the gate of that city, and you shall stone them to death with stones, the young woman because she did not cry out in the city, and the man because he humbled his neighbor's wife" (Deuteronomy 22:23).

There are several significant factors found in this portion of God's Word.

> ➢ The young woman is a virgin.
> ➢ She is betrothed or engaged to a husband.
> ➢ Notice that the betrothed is his wife.

The betrothal or engagement was equivalent in legal status to a marriage ceremony, but cohabitation would follow at a later appointed time.

The symbolical marriage in Hosea implies a perfect marriage from the perspective of the husband. This engagement is built upon righteousness, justice, loving-kindness, mercy and faithfulness. Any man who builds his marriage on those qualities will have a relationship with his bride that cannot be broken.

And how will the bride respond? She will know the Lord.

Hosea 2:20

The English word translated *know* in verse twenty needs some explanation. It comes from the Hebrew word *yada*.

The Hebrew word *yada* is also used in the Bible to describe sexual relations between a husband and wife. "Now Adam knew his wife and she conceived and bore Cain" (Genesis 4:1).

Hosea's inspired message says, "And you shall know the Lord." The word *know* implies a unique intimate relationship with God. The word *you* refers to the true church, which is made up of God's people past, present, and future.

The child of God shall know the Lord in an exceedingly intimate way. It is a marriage made in heaven forever.

To put that in terms of your own eternal estate it means the soul is united to Jesus Christ by faith. The betrothal is exceedingly sacred and eternally secure.

It is a righteous betrothal because in spite of sin, rebellion, and waywardness, the righteousness of Jesus Christ is accounted to the soul of an unrighteous sinner. It is the sacrifice of Jesus Christ that satisfies God's justice. Consequently the knowledge of God increases and His love and mercy overwhelms the justified sinner.

The greatest comfort and joy that a Christian may have

is the knowledge that God will always, throughout eternity, be faithful to His church collectively and to His child individually.

Every Christian wants to have a permanent relationship with God. Some people are very lonely and would desire even a temporary friend, but deep down everyone wants a more permanent relationship.

The most exciting time in a young couple's life is when they are engaged to each other. Seldom will either find fault with the other. How many would like an engagement like that to last forever? Is there such a thing as a permanent eternal engagement? I believe it is!

The Bible teaches that there is a courtship leading to a permanent engagement.
Hosea 2:14-15

God uses such beautiful romantic language to describe the courtship. "I will allure her."

The word *allure* must be considered in light of the following biblical text. The New King James Version is, "If a man *entices* a virgin who is not betrothed..." The New American Standard is "If a man *seduces* a virgin who is not engaged..." (Exodus 22:16).

The same Hebrew word translates as *allure*, *entice*, or *seduce*. It means to win over or to attract.

God attracted his people into the wilderness. Why does

God take His people into a wilderness? There are several reasons.

The wilderness is a place you may go to face the trials of this life and afterward go into the Promised Land. The child of God is a sojourner traveling to the place of eternal peace.

The wilderness is a lonely place, but a lonely place is necessary so God can speak to your soul. The wilderness is the place where the soul can repent and believe in the power and holiness of God. It was in the wilderness when Moses saw the burning bush and it was there that Moses experienced the presence and holiness of God.

Has God lead you into the wilderness? Then be thankful.

Every Christian should ask a deeper and more important question. Did God's courtship lead you into a permanent relationship with Him? If the answer is yes, then you will find your new home in the new heavens and the new earth.

However, the wilderness is a bad place without the favorable presence of God. Who wants a permanent home in the wilderness?

Christians want to have assurance that God and His promises are forever. The confirmation of a permanent engagement is the joy of the soul.
Hosea 2:16-18

The engagement will be confirmed by purification. All the temptations, all the false gods and all the promises of the evil one will be remembered no more when God purifies His people and renews His covenant with His people.

Purification comes because God does the work of betrothal. When God says, "I will" it is a statement of permanent reality.
Hosea 2:19

It is because of God's mercy that His children have the promise of a permanent engagement.
Hosea 2:21-23

This symbolizes a marriage that can never be annulled. The cosmic harmony expressed in this text characterizes God's power and glory in the world. This world represents the wilderness in which all Christians sojourn.

The sojourn through this wilderness may exercise your faith, but by the mercy and compassion of God you will enter into the Promised Land.

You will make it through this wilderness by seeking the Lord while He may be found.

The great hope of the church is to hear God say:
You are my people.

And the church shall say:
You are my God!

The engagement to be the Lord's bride forever is the joy of every Christian.

May God grace you in that eternal marriage!

Amen.

Proof of God's Love

Hosea 3:1-5

The symbolism found in the first three chapters of Hosea is a kind of autobiography. Perhaps it is best described as a prophetic autobiography.

In chapter one Hosea married Gomer at God's command and they had children.

In chapter two Gomer committed adultery and Hosea divorces Gomer.

Now in chapter three the Lord commissions Hosea to demonstrate the immensity of God's love.

"Go show your love to your wife."
(New International Version)
Hosea 3:1

The Bible student and teacher must be careful at this juncture. God's law is abundantly clear about this matter of remarriage to a divorced wife except for adultery. Read Deuteronomy 24:1-4 for an explanation. Hosea's remarriage to Gomer is a source of great debate among theologians.

The debate by the great theological minds through the centuries is whether or not Hosea actually remarried Gomer or was this a parabolic figure of speech. Since this is a brief commentary, I will make a brief comment.

It is not important to keep up with the detail in all these earthly events because they ultimately translate into heavenly symbolism. It is necessary to keep in mind that these experiences of Hosea have analogical value. The physical aspect helps explain the spiritual relationship between God and His people.

This marriage divorce remarriage in the life of Hosea is an appropriate analogy to the relationship God has with His people.

"The children of Israel look to other gods" is a theme throughout Hosea's message. The fundamental sin of the human race is to go after other gods. Adam and Eve were not content with a perfect world. Satan, the chief false god, deceived Eve to believe there was something better than perfection. People love false gods because false gods are crafty, charming, and convincing. People love themselves and their false gods because they pretend to be independent beings. It is sad for them, because independence is a characteristic that belongs only to God.

God loved the northern kingdom even though she rebelled against God, even though she turned to idol worship and was unfaithful to God. This is the analogy of Hosea's marriage to Gomer. The analogy has eternal consequences, but the physical acts are temporary and will disappear like the morning dew.

The analogy of Hosea's divorce must be understood in light of God's relationship to His people. The Old Testament church adopted false gods to worship. After numerous warnings to repent, over a long period of time, God punished the northern kingdom by sending her into exile at the hand of the Assyrian Army. It was like God divorced His church.

The historical context is important because from 950 B.C. to 722 B.C. the Old Testament church consisted of the northern kingdom (Israel) and the southern kingdom (Judah). Hosea's prophetic spoken ministry was in and to the northern kingdom between 760 B.C. and 722 B.C. The southern kingdom survived the Assyrian captivity and exile in 722 B.C. Hosea's spoken message was written and communicated to the southern kingdom. The message was the northern kingdom suffered this tragedy because of their rebellion, idolatry, and unfaithfulness. However, God is merciful and there is hope.

The church in the southern kingdom should learn from Hosea's symbolic experience. They should take note that God's justice against infidelity is forthcoming to the southern kingdom unless they repent.

The church today faces the possibility of judgment, because she has departed from the Word of God as the ruling principle in faith and life. The way to avoid the impending judgment is to avoid practices that bring judgment on the church.

Another prophet spoke similar to Hosea. "Thus says the

Lord" are the words spoken by Amos the prophet, but obviously he was merely the mouth piece for God.

> For three transgressions of Judah and for four, I will not turn away its punishment, because they have despised the law of the Lord, and have not kept His commandments. Their lies lead them astray – lies which their fathers followed" (Amos 2:4).

A price must be paid to redeem God's children from condemnation. No doubt the purchase price Hosea paid for his second wife reminds Christians of the purchase price the Lord Jesus Christ paid for them. Who would pay such a price for a prostitute? Could it be said that God loves the unlovely?

Hosea 3:2

Even though God's children have been redeemed they are not free of sin and suffering. Hosea's prophecy is especially given to God's children who struggle against sin in their lives and for those who suffer.

God is patient and longsuffering. Notice God said, "Go Again."

God will let His rebellious children go their way until they come to their senses.

Hosea 3:4

Punishment to the church in the Old Testament was exile; for the northern kingdom in 722 B.C. and the southern kingdom in 586 B.C. God gave them what they wanted. He let His children become slaves to their false gods. God's punishment comes when He withholds his blessings as He did to the Old Testament church.

God withheld His blessing in the Old Testament Church so that the New Testament church may understand and avoid the same mistakes.

God warned the northern kingdom that she would be "many days without king or prince." The time would come when the Old Testament church would be without leadership. They were without a temporal king whose model was King David. All the kings from the time of the divided kingdom in 950 B.C. to 586 B.C. were compared to King David. Read 2 Chronicles 29:1 to see how the kings of Israel are compared to David. After the reign of King David the Old Testament Church had leadership, but it was the wrong kind of leadership.

They were also without a spiritual king, not because God had left them, but because they had left God.

The loss of leadership in the church is punishment because it reminds godly people of the need for godly leaders.

The people of the northern kingdom had long departed from following the sacrificial ceremonial laws reminding them of God's pardon and forgiveness of sin. Instead they sacrificed to all kinds of fertility gods and worshipped every kind of idol. To deprive God's people of the opportunity to worship is the worst kind of punishment. The guilt, shame, and misery of sin leave the sinner destitute of peace.

The people were without the *ephod* and *teraphim*. The ephod was a garment worn by a priest prescribed by Old Testament ceremonial laws. The *teraphim* were personal gods and were consulted because of their alleged divine powers. The *ephod* was proper for worship. The *teraphim* were false gods. The *ephod* and *teraphim* are outward forms of religious worship. To worship either or both of them is like going through the ritual without affecting the heart.

God punished the Old Testament church by taking away their leadership and their worship.

If God withholds his blessing, especially his spiritual blessing, it is time for an accountability checkup.

Ask yourself these questions. Did Christ suffer, spill His blood and die for those He called to Himself? Am I one of those He called? If so, am I showing the work of the spirit or the work of the flesh?

Are the works of the flesh in control? Is pride, lust or covetousness in control? If so then you live with "hatred, envy, murder, strife, deceit, evil-mindedness," which causes the heart of the soul to be undiscerning, unloving, unforgiving and unmerciful (Galatians 5:19-21).

If any of those things are in control of your life or live comfortably in the church, then God's heavy hand may come in the form of punishment. God may punish His people, but that does not mean He does not love them.

God's punishment is proof that He loves His children, but it is not the desired manner to receive his love. Christians much prefer God's favorable blessing as proof of His love.

Hoses 3:5

The word *afterward* may be translated as *latter days* and is the warning of the coming exile. During the exile there was no leadership and no worship.

The absence of godly leadership and the absence of worship is a severe form of punishment. However, if they are truly God's children they will always return to Him.

The evangelical church describes this return in terms of a reformation.

A return of godly leadership always begins with Jesus Christ as the head and the king of the church.

Godly leadership is always a mark of God's blessing. It is proof of God's love for His children. Godly leadership is a mark of a healthy church. The return of godly worship is proof of God's blessing and therefore proof of God's love for His children.

Christians must not carelessly or willfully neglect or forsake their duty to worship. When it comes to worship, they must obey Holy Scripture without any distortion or blemish.

God's blessing of leadership and worship comes when the church seeks His leadership and endeavors to worship in spirit and truth.

The proof of God's love is evident in the mind, heart, and soul of His people as long as they follow the Lord. When the prophet says, "They shall fear the Lord" he means that they were miserable as long as they were under his punishment, but returning to Him and submitting to Him brought real happiness and joy.

The goodness of the gospel is sufficient proof of God's love to the sinner. It is in the goodness of the gospel that sinners find pardon and forgiveness.

The church collectively will receive, to a greater or lesser degree, God's punishment or His blessing.

The proof of God's love is when a good God demonstrates His love to bad people. Do you believe this? Then return to God.

Spiritual Poverty

Hosea 4:1-19

The Word of the Lord is not very popular in our relativistic age. A short Bible reading once a week is the best that many professingChristians are able to handle.

There have been times of reform and revival in the history of God's people. It is the discovery or rediscovery of the Word of the Lord that ushers in reformation and revival.

About forty years before the fall of the southern kingdom in 586 B.C., Josiah the king of the southern kingdom restored worship in Jerusalem. While the priests were cleaning out the temple they found the Word of the Lord (Read the whole story in 2 Chronicles 34.)

The king demanded the public reading of the Word of the Lord and when the king heard the words from the Bible he tore his clothes. Tearing his clothes was an expression of grief. Has the Word of God ever gripped you that way?

The leaders in the Old Testament church discovered the Word of the Lord and they rediscovered its meaning and application to their lives.

Even though that was over twenty five hundred years ago, it should stimulate the church for renewal in this present generation.

The 18th century Puritans rediscovered the Word of the Lord. It was in the Word of God that they found the regulative principle. Although not frequently used today, the regulative principle means exactly what it says. They saw the Bible as the ruling principle that explained life and regulated the behavior for the Christian church.

The church today needs to hear the Word of the Lord. She ought to rediscover the regulative principle. The best place to begin is by listening to the Word of God. The prophet Hosea commands God's people to "Hear." **Hosea 4:1**

It may sound strange that the Bible commands God's people to "hear the Word of the Lord." If the Word of God is not central to the life of the believer, then self becomes the central aspect of existence. The deification of self begins when men and women forget God and spend their time thinking about themselves. The more they forget about God the more they think about themselves. Paul warned the church that it would happen.

Leading men and women back to God is difficult. The sin of turning away from God must be challenged by the Word of the Lord. Hosea's message was and still is the Word of God.

Sometimes it is necessary to take legal action to get the attention of a law breaker. God sued the Old Testament church or as Scripture describes it, "the Lord brings a charge against the inhabitants of the land." Before you charge God with being harsh and unjust, it is important to remember that God sent the preacher Hosea to warn them of the impending danger.

God calls preachers to warn believers and unbelievers of their sin and offer them the hope of salvation. Moses, Samuel, all the prophets, Peter, Paul and especially the Lord the Jesus preached the law that condemns and the gospel that saves. Ezekiel clarifies any misunderstanding relative to the subject of preaching. (Read and study Ezekiel 3:16-19; 33:1-7.)

The continual preaching and teaching of the Word of the Lord has two effects.

> ➢ When God threatens his children with His righteous judgment, they ought to repent and confess their sin. They should have a healthy fear of the Lord (Deuteronomy 4:10).

> ➢ When unbelievers hear the Word of the Lord they harden their hearts and make every effort to quench the power of truth.

In either case the Lord takes away any pretext for ignorance and wounds the conscience with his warnings.

The tragedy is that many church members have not

heard the Word of the Lord. Some congregations have only heard a small watered down portion of the Word of the Lord. They have heard the words of men rather than the Word of the Lord.

Unfortunately some professing Christians, who have heard the truth from the Word of God preached for years, maybe even decades, still want milk rather than solid food (1 Corinthians 3:1-4).

The prophets and priests were acting foolishly and rejecting the Word of the Lord.
Hosea 4:5

Likewise the people rejected the Word of the Lord.
Hosea 4:9

The application of this text is wide and deep. The contemporary church must engage with the full counsel of God to prevent corrupt worship, unbiblical evangelism and programs without any biblical basis. If the church rejects or compromises the Word of God, then she will promote her own private agenda.

Unless the church turns to the Word of the Lord, spiritual poverty will overtake her.

There are three primary factors that affect spiritual poverty.

> ➤ Man's standing before God
> ➤ Man's ability to think
> ➤ Man's moral condition

The unbeliever not only lives in spiritual poverty, he or she is spiritually bankrupt. The saved sinner on the other hand has a renewed mind and will. Having a renewed mind the Bible comes alive with truth and a passion for truth.

Man's ability to think and reason is directly related to a biblical belief system, which will prevent spiritual poverty. A belief system is built on a person's ability to think. It is also known as rational thought. God created humans with the ability to think.

God gives Christian human beings the ability to think about spiritual things in a positive sense. They are able to believe the Word of God.

Hosea gave three reasons for the spiritual poverty found in the church, both the Old Testament and New Testament.

- No truth - Think about this: God is truth. God cannot lie. The Devil is the father of lies (John 8:44).

- No mercy - Mercy is the mother of truth and knowledge.

- No knowledge - The knowledge of God is associated with the spiritual condition of man (Romans 1:20).

When the prophet Hosea said, "there is no truth in the land," he must mean there was a breakdown in relationships. Unless a person has a right relationship with God, there is no interest in truth. Furthermore bad relationships among people is the cause of the lack of integrity (Romans 1:18).

Truth is a necessary condition to intelligent human discourse.

What if our words are not truthful? People would be unable to have sensible communication because everything would be in a state of confusion. If words of are not based on truth, the culture will soon devolve into chaos.

What if our promises are not truthful? Not only will broken promises break down communications, broken promises create animosity and dissension.

What if our witness is not truthful? When applied to the Christian religion, false witness is the worst form of sacrilege. Jesus used another word for false witness. It was hypocrisy.

It is the duty of every Christian to be truthful in word, promise and witness.

The word of the Lord goes on to say that there was no mercy in the land.

It was the duty of the priest to mediate between the people and God. Since the priests had set their hearts to sin against God, the mercy ministry ceased to function.

Hosea explains it in terms of the priest who catered to the desires of the people.
Hosea 4:8-9

One of the primary reasons for the gross spiritual poverty in the church is because "there is no knowledge of God in the land."

In the day of Hosea, as in our day, there were two reasons that the knowledge of God was not in the land.
Hosea 4:6

Preachers are called by God to be leaders. They are supposed to lead God's people through this wilderness into the Promised Land. What the people need is the Word of God, not the personal agenda of the preacher. Unfortunately congregations are leading the preachers into darkness, and the preachers are gladly following.

God said, "My people are destroyed for a lack of knowledge." The priest ignored God's law and so did the people. The priest plunged headlong into idolatry and the people gladly followed.

The destruction of the people is not the annihilation of the people. The destruction refers to God's judgment and discipline applied to His church.

The lack of the knowledge of God has several levels.

> ➤ The soul without knowledge of God is a starving soul doomed to perish.

➢ The soul with a false knowledge of God is a soul without any hope.

➢ The soul with a limited and disinterested knowledge of God fails to grasp the beauty of God's holiness and true Christian worship.

The more Christians attempt to plead ignorance before God, the more they are intimidated by His power, dignity and glory.

The passion and desire should be to gain the knowledge of God according to Holy Scripture.

Not only will a biblical belief system prevent spiritual poverty, a biblical ethic will also prevent spiritual poverty.
Hosea 4:2

When a belief system falls apart, so will the morals of the believer. If truth, mercy, and knowledge of God disappears then you can expect cursing, lying, killing, stealing and adultery to increase. Ignore the truth and the ignorance of God's holiness will prevail.

Elevate the sinfulness of man and then every conceivable crime against God will prevail in the land.

Show me a Christian who has no use for truth and I will show you a Christian who has little respect for the law of God.

If Christians expect to avoid spiritual poverty, they

must be willing to believe biblical doctrine and obey the law of God.

If they do not believe and obey God, He will give them what they want, that is to worship false gods.
Hosea 4:16

In fact false gods will consume them.
Hosea 4:17-19

I urge you to make godliness the great end in your life.

I urge you to hold fast to God's truth.

I urge you to increase in your sanctification.

I urge you to give attention to verse fifteen. Let me summarize it for you. Don't do what former generations have done that has caused this exile.

Let your spiritual poverty be forever removed.

Where is God When I'm in Trouble?

Hosea 5:1-15

When God speaks through His Word, it is important to know the original audience.

So far in Hosea the prophet addressed the audience as "my people" and therefore God expresses collective ownership of His people.

In Chapter four the prophet said "Hear the word of the Lord, you Children of Israel." An individual member in the congregation may think that it is non-specific nebulous language and therefore not applicable to every individual in the church.

Every member in the congregation ought to have an interest in the Word of God. The idea the some church members are not under the authority of Holy Scripture is ridiculous.

This text corrects any such silly notion.
Hosea 5:1

Notice that it is not generic language. The Lord speaks through the prophet Hosea specifically to certain individuals in the church, yet together they collectively make up the whole church.

The priests are commanded to hear the Word of God. The application today would include pastors, preachers, and teachers. The House of Israel must take heed to the Word of God, which includes everyone in the congregation. The house of the King applies to other church leaders.

The priest, congregation, and king contributed to the national guilt in Israel. No one in those categories could escape what God was about to say, because it comes in the form of a command. This commandment must be interpreted in light of the full counsel of God. The command to *hear* applies to the entire human race. Those who are born again by the power of the Holy Spirit have the ability to *understand* the Word of God. Unbelievers do not.

The first command is hear. It carries with it the force of an injunction. It is not an asking command like "open the window" but a command that says, "do it or suffer consequences!"

The second command is "take heed." It is an injunction, but the force of this verb indicates that God will cause you to take heed.

The third command is "Give ear." The emphatic nature of God's commandment is like screaming to the church leaders to pay attention to the Word of God. Disregard for these two little words explain how the evangelical church as whole turned to liberal theology and unbelief. She refused to give ear to the word of God.

These three very powerful commands intensify so as to reflect God's sovereign authority over His people and His leaders.

God's people in every generation hear the Word of God. **Hosea 5:2**

What does Hosea's message mean for churches throughout the world today? What does it mean for the local church? What does it mean to every individual person in the church?

I "rebuke them all" means the same thing today as it did the day that Hosea uttered these words. God's Word stands firm. Consider it a privilege to be rebuked by the Lord God almighty.

"He who is often rebuked and hardens his neck, will suddenly be destroyed, and that without remedy" (Proverbs 29:1).

God rebukes His people through the preaching of the Word of God. It is a sad commentary, but there is a misunderstanding about the purpose of preaching. Preaching is not teaching. It is not communicating facts that call for personal application. Preaching is not a preacher's opinion about religious matters

Preaching is God's way of communicating the truth about His holiness and justice. Preaching the wicked depraved nature of men and women must precede the good news of God's saving grace. The depraved sinner can be reconciled to God through Jesus Christ by the power of the Holy Spirit.

I expect many go to church (a misnomer in itself) hoping that God will help them with some kind of difficulty or problem they have experienced or expect to experience.

Christians ought to examine themselves before they go to worship. If the spirit of harlotry prevails in worship, God will not be present in a favorable sense.

When you face the trials of this life do you ever say to yourself "I wonder why God let it happen to me?" Christians struggle to understand the mysterious nature of God's providence. The question that was, is, and will continue to be asked is, "where is God when I'm in trouble?"

God is the same "yesterday, today and forever." His essence and character is unchangeable. He does not move away to a new location (Hebrews 13:8).

The resolve of every Christian ought to be:

- If the sin in my life bugs me,
- If my worship is empty,
- If I am troubled with my portion in life,
- I should never ask the question,
- ➤ "Where is God when I'm in trouble?"

The cause of all trouble in this life is sin. The source of sin is from the sinner (Romans 7:5; 8:5).

The sin of pride will cause the child of God to stumble. **Hosea 5:5**

What is the sin of pride? It is the elevation of self-esteem to the degree that one's opinion becomes more important than the precepts of God.

There is a proper self-esteem whereby Christians recognize their abilities as a gift of God. This is very different than the notorious arrogance of the self-love concept.

Hosea does not mention the specific sin of pride, but it probably has to do with the Israelites contempt for instruction. God had already made it clear that "My people are destroyed for lack of knowledge" (Hosea 4:6).

The sin of pride appears to be connected with "strange children" in Hosea's preaching. **Hosea 5:7**

Scripture does not reveal the pedigree of these children. The New King James Version refers to them as *pagan* children. The term adequately describes children coming from unfaithful covenant breaking parents. Therefore, the strange children did not know God. The parents trained the children to worship false gods. This should provoke serious thought for Christians!

Hosea probably makes this comment to warn the church that there is no future for unfaithful professors of religion.

The northern kingdom of Israel was economically prosperous. Prosperity may cause the sin of pride to raise its ugly head. Pride rejects the knowledge of God and embraces the gods of pleasure. Pride causes the heart to become hard and pride takes away the fear of God.

People stumble in their sins and then blame God by asking, "Where is God when I'm in trouble?"

The presence of God in worship will depend on the nature of worship. Is it true worship or false worship?
Hosea 5:6

The Israelites thought they could pacify God by offering Him an abundance of burnt-offerings.

God expects spiritual worship and it must be offered in spirit and truth.

If Christians think that they can appease God with ceremonies, ritual, and liturgy, they will find themselves worshipping a false god. The true and living God will not be present for false worship.

Pride leads to false worship and false worship rejects the authority and sovereignty of God.
Hosea 5:10

Where is God When I'm in Trouble?

In ancient near eastern cultures natural divisions such as river beds, streams, or edges of valleys were used to mark property lines. In the absence of natural divisions, stones would be placed to mark property lines. It was unlawful to move those landmarks.

When pride and false worship prevails, the inclination is to remove the landmarks God has given to His children (Job 24:2; Isaiah 10:13).

God gives His children the inspired infallible Word from His own mouth. It is a landmark. It is dangerous, both temporally and eternally, to move it, change it or ignore it.

God has given the church His law to be like a fence. It is a landmark that reveals God's own property.

The metaphor of the landmark is a reminder of God's boundaries. When Christians take away His boundaries they find themselves in turmoil and confusion.

If anyone tries to remove God's landmarks He "will pour out His wrath on them like water."

The question is not "Where is God when I'm in trouble?"

However, there are several questions every Christian should ask and answer.

Has my pride and arrogance led to false worship?

Has my false worship caused me to reject the authority and sovereignty of God?

The correct answer is return to the Lord.
Hosea 5:15

The afflictions of the depraved nature will drive Christians to seek the face of God. Christians will submit to His justice. They will love His holiness. They will desire His mercy.

Not only will the children of God seek Him, they will earnestly seek Him especially during the trials of life.

Suffering and oppression will cause God's people to seek His face.

The Christian worldview recognizes the trials and temptations that are sometimes in great abundance. The Bible calls Christians to engage with one another so that a brother or sister in Christ many overcome trials and temptations. Although there is a time to minister to unbelievers, it is urgent to minister to believers. Help them return to the Lord.

They will seek Him in Jesus Christ whose blood has been shed for God's children. I commend you to repent by trusting Christ alone, by faith alone, to glory of God alone.

Then the question will no longer need to be asked: Where is God when I'm in trouble?

Practical Rules in Religious Worship

Hosea 6:1-11

Hosea prophesied for about forty years in the northern kingdom during which time there were seven different kings. It was a time of political turmoil and intrigue. Some of the kings were even murdered by their successor. Read 2 Kings Chapters 14 through 17 for a more thorough historicity during this period.

Everyday life during the prophecy of Hosea was, in principle, the same as today. Some of the words found in 2 Kings, Hosea, and other prophets sound very much like our nation and church. Israel enjoyed prosperity and thought that all religions were equally important. Prosperity is wonderful, but consider all the evil that often accompanies it. The Old Testament church with all their wealth was content to live and worship contrary to the Word of God.

Syncretism is a word that Christians should learn because it describes the mixing of all kinds of religious views into one. It was the nucleus of Israel's false worship. Immorality and false worship are Satan's most enticing venues to persuade God's children to depart from God's plan for life and worship.

Immorality is the result of making all decisions based

on personal preferences. If words are meaningless, then moral objectivity will cease. Internal political strife in the state is the result of abandoning truth, order, and justice.

Israel, as a body politic and the Old Testament church, had lost the fear of being over-taken by the enemy. Assyria sounded so far away. The talk on the street was probably along the lines of "surely God will not allow the Assyrian heathens to overtake us." The headlines and editorials in all the newspapers in every city would affirm the goodness of the people and the northern kingdom. Sounds like Christianity in the United States.

Preachers like Hosea warned against complacency and disregard for God's word. Hosea preached a sermon that said, "judgment is coming and you will suffer, but there is hope."

Hosea's message is replete with warnings from God.

> ➤ I will no longer have mercy on the house of Israel (Hosea 1:4).
> ➤ I will not be your God (Hosea 1:8).
> ➤ I will punish her (Hosea 2:13).
> ➤ God will remove worship (Hosea chapter 3).
> ➤ I will punish them for their ways (Hosea 4:9).
> ➤ I will pour out My wrath on them like water (Hosea 5:10).

God was angry because the people who professed to be His people loved individualism and democracy more than the sovereignty of God. Keep in mind that democracy simply means "people rule" or maybe a more accurate rendering would be "the mob rules."

If God's people would have read their Bibles they would have known what happened during the period of the Judges. "Every man did what was right in his own eyes" (Judges 17:6).

The preacher, Hosea, offers a solution to this problem. The Lord speaking through the prophet Hosea issues this commandment: "Come! Let us return to the Lord." **Hosea 6:1-3**

The Lord commands His children to return to Him, which obviously implies the people professing faith in their loving heavenly Father had departed from the Lord.

Departing from the Lord reminds me of a child saying to his father: "Daddy I don't want to be your child. I'm leaving home!"

Why would a helpless child want to depart from such a wonderful, generous, and loving Father?

The word often used to describe "a departure from the Lord" is *backslide*.

The word *backslide* in the modern church is different than the way Hosea used the word backslide." The concept known as backsliding in the contemporary church has roots in the unbiblical teaching of 19th and 20th century revivalism.

There are two prominent errors that came out of those two centuries of teaching. One is perfectionism and the other is fundamentalism.

The perfectionist refers to the term *backslide* to describe someone who loses his or her salvation because of living an immoral life.

The fundamentalist on the other hand refers to the term *backslide* to describe a Christian who becomes a second class Christian because of a moral failure. They are nicknamed carnal Christians.

These errors are unbiblical views of backsliding. Although the Bible does not give a clear definition of backsliding it does say "The backslider in heart will be filled with his own ways" (Proverbs 14:14).

Therefore, backsliding is the result of every man doing what is right in his own eyes.

All Christians are backsliders in one sense, because they all have the remnant of sin in their hearts to one degree or another. As they grow in sanctification they will be less inclined to backslide.

Backsliding or departing from the Lord may occur, but Christians are marked by the distinction that they will always determine to return to the Lord.

The prophet says "let us return to the Lord." Who is *us*? **Hosea 6:1**

God calls the whole church to return in faith and repentance. No one escapes from this call to return to the Lord (Hosea 5:1).

Not everyone had turned away from the Lord, but Hosea used hyperbole to make his point. Hyperbole is merely the use of an exaggerated statement to make a point.

The Lord always has a remnant of His people. The Lord told Elijah that not every knee bows to Baal (1 Kings 19:18).

Hosea simply states that every class of people in every part of society had departed from the Lord.

What does it mean to depart from the Lord? The national departure from the Lord included the civil, social, and political life of God's people. God warned His people not to go to Assyria or Egypt for protection from their enemies.

Hosea 7:11

Christians ought to ponder the implications and the explicit danger of making ungodly covenants.

Based on twenty five years of ministry experience, I would suggest that most Christians believe that moral failures are the primary reason that people depart from the Lord.

They say backsliding occurs when a person violates one

of the Ten Commandments, especially one of the last six commandments.

If the words immoral behavior enter into a conversation many Christians think it is about sexual misconduct. Such ideas are a result of biblical ignorance and fraudulent teaching in the church. It is immoral behavior to disobey any of the hundreds of commandments found in Holy Scripture. I believe the worst kind of immoral behavior is to violate the first commandment. "You shall have no other gods before Me" (Exodus 20:3).

Immoral behavior comes from the sin nature. When God says, "no other gods before me" it is just as immoral to break that commandment as it is to commit adultery. In fact spiritual adultery is just as bad if not worse that physical adultery. God certainly punished the Old Testament congregation far more severely for spiritual adultery than for physical adultery.

Hosea used several metaphors to describe immoral behavior.

> ➢ The transgression of the covenant (Hosea 6:7).
> ➢ The city of evildoers (Hosea 6:8).
> ➢ Bands of robbers (Hosea 6:9).
> ➢ The horrible thing (Hosea 6:10).

They all reflect immoral characteristics, but immoral behavior is only one aspect of irreverence toward God.

Immoral behavior will always affect ones relationship

with God, relationship with other people, and ones attitude toward worship.

If Christians ignore the law of God and embrace immoral behavior, their worship becomes mere ritual and liturgy.

If the correction of immoral behavior is the purpose of worship, then worship is nothing more than man-centered moralism.

It would benefit the church for its members to know a couple of words that shape religious worship.

Antinomianism is a word that literally means *against the law*. When Christians make immoral behavior a way of life, deny its presence, and do no repent they are acting against the law of God. When that happens worship becomes self-centered.

Moralism is a word that literally means a person lives such a righteous life that there is no need to worship God.

Do you see the danger in both of these religious views? The object of worship is distorted. God must be the object of worship.

Hosea gives the church some practical rules for religious worship. There are moral principles in these rules, but the moral principles are not the center of attention.

The first rule in religious worship is to remain faithful to God in worship.
Hosea 6:6

The word mercy comes from the Hebrew word *chesed,* which is translated lovingkindness 176 times in the Old Testament. Mercy in this text is relative to lovingkindness.

The Bible reveals to the child of God that the "Lord is longsuffering and abundant in mercy [lovingkindness]" (Numbers 14:18). The "earth is full of the mercy [lovingkindness] of the Lord" (Psalm 33:5).

The mercy of God is at the forefront of human existence. The Bible clearly teaches "you shall love the Lord your God with all your heart, with all your soul, with all your strength, and with your entire mind..." (Luke 10:27).

To the degree that you love God, then to that same degree you can worship "with all your heart, with all your soul, with all your strength, and with all your mind."

Jesus quotes Hosea, "I desire mercy and not sacrifice" on two occasions (Hosea 6:6).

The first reference is the call of Matthew the tax collector. The Pharisees (the religious leaders of that day) condemned Jesus for drinking and eating with tax collectors and sinners. Then Jesus told them to "Go and learn what this means: I desire mercy and not sacrifice" (Matthew 9:13).

The next reference was when the Pharisees confronted Jesus because he violated their unbiblical man-made rules about the Sabbath. Jesus said to the Pharisees: "I say to you that in this place there is One greater than the temple. But if you had known what this means, I desire mercy and not sacrifice you would not have condemned the guiltless" (Matthew 12:7).

The Lord Jesus Christ called the Pharisees children of Satan even though they were meticulous in their ritualistic worship, but it was dead ritualism which was loathsome to the Lord (John 8:44; Matthew 15:1-9). They were *antinomian*, against God's law, on one hand; they also practiced *moralism*. It is the worst form of contradiction which makes their worship absolutely worthless.

It was empty worship, because their hearts were empty of lovingkindness. The Word of God teaches that a bad heart produces bad motives (Matthew 12:34).

Unfortunately it seems that many professors of Christ practice outward religious worship to accommodate bad motives.

Sacrifice follows faithfulness. Sacrifice does not precede faithfulness and sacrifice is not a substitute for faithfulness. Christians may remain faithful to God in worship if they demonstrate their faith by loving God and their neighbor. When God's people assemble to worship Him it is not acceptable unless they have a right relationship with God through the Lord Jesus Christ by the power of the Holy Spirit. Also worship is not acceptable if the worshipper has not forgiven his or her neighbor and been forgiven by his or her neighbor.

The second rule in religious worship is to worship with the knowledge of God.
Hosea 6:6

Hosea sounds just like a redundant preacher. He just says the same thing over and over again. God inspired Hosea's prophecy, so it seems that the people need to hear the same thing over and over again. God had already spoken to the people through the mouth of Hosea and said, "There is no truth or mercy or knowledge of God in the land" (Hosea 4:1).

Ignorance of God is especially a lamentable evil in worship. God created His children to worship Him. His children, the church of God, are not able to worship Him if they do not have the knowledge of Him as it is revealed in Scripture.

It is the duty of every Christian to know what the Bible teaches about God's character (what He is) and to know what the Bible teaches about His conduct (what He does). If Christians are destitute of the knowledge of God, they place themselves in a perilous state.

Christians ought to practice what they know about God when they gather to worship. God demands truth in everything, especially in worship. For instance, singing hymns that are contrary to the Word of God is like singing a lie to God. For instance one hymn says "Christ emptied himself of all but love." It is simply not true, because if Christ only retained the attribute commonly known as love, it denies His deity. Another hymn says "perfect submission, perfect delight, filled with His goodness." That hymn is an example of Roman Catholic theology. Goodness equals righteousness. Christians are not filled with righteousness. They are declared righteous because of the sacrifice of Christ. These examples show a lack of integrity in interpreting Scripture and applying it to songs used in public worship. For the worshipper it shows a lack of discernment and singing to God something that is not true, which is false worship.

Christians ought to listen carefully and critically to the public reading and preaching of the Word of God. Study the Word of God with as much passion as anything else you do in this life. Always take delight in the use of God's means of grace.

The prophet cries out "return to the Lord." Return to the Lord with true and spiritual worship to overcome the inclination to engage in false and unspiritual worship.

The Lord Jesus Christ came at the proper time so the church might understand the basis for all religious worship. God gives His people practical rules in religious worship.

Mercy must be the first rule in religious worship and

knowledge of God is the second rule in religious worship.

False Hope

Hosea 7:1-16

Hosea made this prophetic announcement for the northern kingdom in the face of an impending crisis.

His prophecy was written so that the southern kingdom and every generation of God's people might know that God always executes justice.

There is hope of restoration for both kingdoms if they repent and return to the Lord.

Christians should study the context of chapter seven to better understand the religious, political, and moral implications for that period of time. A brief survey of 2 Kings 15 reveals the depravation of the religious, political and social life in the northern kingdom. The lust for power was a prominent and public sin. It is not uncommon in the world today even in the church of Jesus Christ.

The prophet Hosea loved God's people in the southern kingdom enough to warn them about the certainty and severity of God's judgment. If the Word of God means anything to Christians today, they must also be aware that the church may face the possibility of God's judgment.

The contemporary church should learn what the Old

Testament church did not learn that God is just. Individual sins as well as the collective sins of the church will provoke God's wrath. The church must learn how to avoid those practices that bring God's judgment.

God calls the individual and the church collectively to repent. The prophet Hosea explains why the Old Testament church failed to repent. First they failed to repent because they did not have the love of God and secondly they had a feeble knowledge of God.
Hosea 6:6

If there is no love and no knowledge of God, the prophet says, "They do not consider in their hearts that I remember all their wickedness."
Hosea 7:2

If there is no love and no knowledge of God, the wicked person does not realize that God remembers his evil deeds (Romans 1:28).

Furthermore God, speaking through the prophet Hosea said, "None among them calls upon Me."
Hosea 7:7

They may have cried out to God, but their motives were selfish and they failed to cry out in repentance.

People tend to ask the wrong question like, "God why are you letting this happen to me" when they should ask "what did I do to deserve God's displeasure."

At the time Hosea prophesied, the nation of Israel enjoyed the prosperity of God's providence, but Israel was without faith.

She wanted international fame and would do anything to have it. When the surrounding nations threatened invasion and Israel faced ultimate destruction, she allowed pride and self-centeredness to control her thinking and her actions.

The corruption that comes from pride and self-centeredness is always destructive, beginning its destructive force in the depth of the soul and always working outward. However, God always knows the hearts of men and that is the reason God said, "None among them calls upon Me."

Man deceives himself into thinking he can handle anything that comes his way. All too often people will say "I'll do this or that" without adding those two important words *deo volente*. Those two little Latin words translated into English are *Lord willing* and although Christians may not say them outwardly, they must always be in the mind of the soul.

Without the blessing and grace of God, people will cheerfully follow their own ways. The Bible says, "everyone did what was right in his own eyes" (Judges 17:6). (I'm aware that I've used this verse several times in this commentary. I believe it is associated with the fundamental sin problem of the human race).

Could it be that the grace of God is not evident in His

church because of false hope? Has the church allowed the world to invade her ranks and dictate to her like it was in the days of old when "everyone did what was right in his own eyes?"

False hope in all the man-made methods and ideas consuming the minds of leaders and laymen translates into the possibility of God's judgment for the church.

The modern church should take heed to God's Word and learn from the prophet Hosea how false hope destroyed the Old Testament church.

False hope will always result in chaos.
Hosea 7:8

This metaphor describes the process of baking bread on a hearth. Place hot coals on the hearth then sweep it clean. Place the flattened dough on the hearth and put hot coals on the hearth around the dough. After a little while the bread cake is turned and the process continues until the bread it done.

Hosea speaks with the kind of language that the people would understand. His message to the Old Testament church was "you are like a cake unturned." One side is done and the other side is raw.

The Bible says Ephraim is a cake unturned. Ephraim represents Israel and Israel represents the church. Ephraim, like the church, was burnt on one side, but doughy on the other side. It might have the appearance of being cooked, but it was an unbaked lump of paste. It was a confusing mixture, just like Ephraim's worship was mixed with false gods.

Ephraim was proud, because of the claim to be God's people. Circumcision distinguished them as God's covenant people outwardly, but inwardly they were covenant breakers. Unfortunately their worship was corrupt and their sacrifices were defective.

So the problem continues in the church today. The church of Jesus Christ must not adopt the ways, ideas, or practices of an ungodly world.

Ephraim mixed false worship with true worship. "Ephraim is a cake unturned." It is false hope to be mixed among the peoples of the world for the purpose of service and worship to the Lord God almighty.

Each week the church ought to assemble as God's people and confess together the need for faith and a call to repentance. They ought to confess and say, "Come, and let us return to the Lord" (Hosea 6:1).

The result of not returning to the Lord is not a pleasant picture. False hope will not only result in chaos, false hope will bring God's punishment on the church.
Hosea 7:11-12

Remember the context is during the reign of King Hoshea (732 B.C - 724 B.C.). He was a vassal king under the rule of Tiglath Pileser, the king of Assyria. King Hoshea was ruthless, irresponsible and under heavy tribute to the Assyrian king and was eventually imprisoned by Shalmaneser, the king of Assyria. King Hoshea's political maneuvering intended to stop tribute payments to Assyria. The prophet used that occasion to remind the Old Testament church that false hope will only lead to God's judgment.

Hosea's message has a metaphor that most anyone will understand. It is about a silly dove, without sense. A dove flies erratically literally darts back and forth. The dove sometimes appears to be senseless.

Like a darting dove, Israel went from one place to the other looking for the best deal to protect them from the aggressor. They failed to base their decisions on the Word of God. If a political connection with Egypt was more expedient than Assyria, then go with Egypt or vice versa.

The Old Testament church ignored God's message of judgment. They should trust God, not Egypt.

> You have seen what I did to the Egyptians, and how I bore you on eagles' wings and brought you to Myself. Now therefore, if you will indeed obey My voice and keep My covenant, then you shall be a special treasure to Me above all people. (Exodus 19:4-5)

Yet God's people acted like gullible brainless doves by going from one place to another looking for deliverance from the enemy, rather than returning to the true and living God.

This metaphor also shows how easy it is to trick a dove. Hunters know that baiting a field for a dove shoot will bring the doves into their sight. Baiting the field deceives the doves into thinking, if they think, that they have a meal, but actually they are going to their destruction.

Deception is Satanic. Beware of deceptive tricks. They lead to false hope. Professing Christians need to replace the false hope with true hope in God's Word.

False hope was the majority report in the Old Testament church during the prophecy of Hosea. *Them*, *they*, and *their*, are the words that define the collective church.
Hosea 7:13-16

> ➢ *They* cried out to God with their mouth, but not their heart.
> ➢ *They* rebelled against God by refusing to believe His word.
> ➢ *They* devise evil against me by worshipping false gods.

"They return, but not to the Most High" is a bit elusive to know precisely what the message conveys. It is possible that they were being deceptive by saying they return, but in reality did not return to the Lord. If the people said or even thought they returned and did not really return, it was nothing more than false hope.

Is it possible for the church to escape this false hope? Hosea gave the answer nearly 2700 yrs ago. Hear the

Word of the Lord and return to the Lord with love for Him and knowledge of Him, so you can serve Him.

Jesus Christ came so that false hope in sacrifice and offerings could be replaced by true hope in Him. False hope is man-made and the product of this world. True hope is God-made and lives in the soul.

I leave you with this beatitude from the apostle Peter:

> Blessed be the God and Father of our Lord Jesus Christ, who according to His abundant mercy has begotten us again to a living hope through the resurrection of Jesus Christ from the dead, to an inheritance incorruptible and undefiled and that does not fade away, reserved in heaven for you, who are kept by the power of God through faith for salvation ready to be revealed in the last time. (1 Peter 1:3 ff)

Live According to God's Word

Hosea 8:1-14

Hosea announced God's message to the church. It would be like one preacher speaking to the entire church in this country. His prophecy included every class of people in the nation of Israel, but every individual may not have been the target of his prophecy.

The message to the congregation was bad news and good news. The bad news was that Hosea believed the church in the northern kingdom was apostate. The word apostate or apostasy is a harsh word in the eyes of many Christians. It most often refers to a complete turning away from the religious views once believed to be true and important. The prophet Jeremiah explains this sad condition. "Why then has this people, Jerusalem, turned away in continual apostasy? They hold fast to deceit, they refuse to return" (Jeremiah 8:5, NASV).

The good news is that God will save His people.
Hosea 2:19-20

Turning away from the Lord is a recurring problem that every generation of God's people must struggle against. The majority of the church may turn away from the Lord. Even though the church may be on a low ebb, God saves a remnant for every generation. For example during the ministry of Elijah there was a general apostasy, but the Lord "reserved seven thousand in Israel, all whose knees have not bowed to Baal, and every mouth that has not kissed him" (1 Kings 19:18).

The sinful heart is the reason people love to offer external worship with pomp and regalia. However, to offer God worship without love and the knowledge of God will end up in apostasy.

Someone may say, "I love the Lord and want to do the Lord's will." God revealed His will for His people in His Word, now commonly known as the Bible.

The Bible is clear on the matter of God's will for His children. By inspiration from God the Apostle Paul wrote and said, "For this is the will of God, your sanctification" (1 Thessalonians 4:3).

Sanctification is the process of a saved sinner growing and maturing as a child of God. The Holy Spirit enables the renewed man or woman to turn from sin and live unto righteousness.

Sanctification is a work of the Holy Spirit so that the moral condition of the saved sinner is brought into conformity with his or her justified legal state before God.

Sanctification is a call to holy living by the power of God so that the child of God may avoid God's hand of wrath.

The message in Hosea is a call to God's people both

individually and collectively to "set the trumpet to your mouth."
Hosea 8:1

The trumpet symbolizes God's warning of His coming judgment. The reason God gives for the coming judgment is that His people broke God's covenant. They rebelled against God's standard for a good relationship.

When God spoke through the mouth of Hosea and said, "they have rebelled against my law" it means they worshipped false gods, violated the Sabbath and broke the other commandments given by God.

It is time for Christians to sound the trumpet, because the church as a whole is perilously close to apostasy.

The Old Testament saints ignored God's warnings. The congregation in the northern kingdom had the Word of God, given to them through the mouth of Hosea. Later the southern kingdom had the Word of God in written form, which we call the Bible.

Unfortunately the Old Testament church disregarded the Word of God and the consequence was contempt for the value of truth.
Hosea 8:12

The Word of God remains "a strange thing" for many professing Christians. They prefer to capture the most recent cultural trend. The increase in postmodern thought and secularism within the church has been one of Satan's most successful ventures over the past fifty years in western civilization.

The inclination to believe that the Bible is a moral roadmap or a compass or a guidebook for successful living is rampant in the church. The Bible is not merely a guidebook; it is the final authority for all of faith and life.

Nearly twenty years ago a preacher from an evangelical church told me that the Bible was not truthful and that one interpretation is just as good as the other. If there are many interpretations of the Bible, then there are many gods. The Old Testament church went after false gods, which ultimately leads to false worship.

The language of the prophet Hosea suggests that the people not only departed from the law of God, but they despised the law of God. To despise the law of God is the same thing as despising the Bible. It was the Old Testament church, the people that professed to be God's people; they considered the Word of God a strange thing. Like the preacher said, "interpret the Bible any way that suits you."

If there is no Word of God, then there is no final authority for faith and life. There is no final authority to know who to worship and how to worship. If there is no final authority then man must be independent so he may worship whomever and however he pleases.

Notice the words of this text, "I have written" which means God is the author of Holy Scripture. If you deny the truth of Scripture then you deny the God who gave that truth.

The truth is that God has written "great things."

Yet the people in the Old Testament church considered these "great things" a "strange thing."

Paul brings "great things" into proper perspective in 2 Timothy 3:14-17.

It is dangerous to reject or despise the Word of God. An angel came to Zacharias and gave Zacharias a promise of a son. Zacharias questioned the angel, who was speaking for God. It was the same as rejection and despite for the truth.

Do you know what happened to Zacharias? The angel said,

> I am Gabriel, who stands in the presence of God, and was sent to speak to you and bring you these glad tidings. But behold, you will be mute and not able to speak until the day these things take place, because you did not believe my words which will be fulfilled in their own time. (Luke 1:8-25)

Let these words "because you did not believe my words" penetrate into your soul.

It becomes easy to despise the Word of God with what I call "but theology."

I believe the Word of God, but..........

I know what the Word of God says, but.........

It becomes easy to despise the Word of God with uncritical acceptance of tradition that is contrary to Holy Scripture.

The solution is to believe the great things God has written in His law, which is the Word of God. Build your world and life view on the sound teaching found in Holy Scripture.

The Old Testament church put on the ugly face of hypocrisy to cover up their rejection of God's word. **Hosea 8:2**

I believe the translation in the New King James Version is dependable, but the translators are not able to give a full explanation of the Hebrew perfect verb translated into English, *will cry*.

The future action depends on the habitual activity of the subject. The subject is Israel and the verb *will cry* expresses the sensational passion of the people. "Israel cried to me" is a theme found throughout Scripture (Judges 3:9; Psalm 18:41; Micah 3:4).

How many times have you cried out to God? Job says, "the souls of the wounded cry out" (Job 24:12). "I cry out to You, but You do not answer me" (Job 30:20). Individual Christians and the church collectively cry out.

The Lord said, "Israel will cry to Me, My God, we know You."

The language indicates that the people felt a sense of accomplishment by saying those few words.

They thought their personal experiences reflected the truth of God and how they were to worship Him. Nothing could have been further from the truth.

Here are a few examples of how experience captivated the minds of the Old Testament saints.

> ➢ They made idols for themselves (Hosea 8:4).
> ➢ They sow the wind is a figure of speech. It indicates that they appeared to worship the true God, but it is appearance only and is not really worship at all (Hosea 8:7).
> ➢ They have gone up to Assyria (Hosea 8:9).

Their man-made ideas replaced God's truth. People who worship false gods will devote themselves to idol worship. They have great confidence in false worship because of their experience. Since false gods are man-made they are sensational and become part of the human experience.

It is very popular to follow tradition in the church. People tend to believe what they hear particularly if it lines up with their own personal experience and world view.

If the old saying "we've always done it this way" is not

God's way according to God's Word, then look for God's judgment to descend upon the church.

If Christians say, "everybody else does it this way" and it is not God's way according to God's Word, then look for God's judgment to descend upon the church.

Although Hosea's message was and still is to the whole church, individual Christians are not exempt from God's judgment. If someone works against God's will according to His Word, then sooner or later and it may be later, perhaps much later, God's judgment will prevail.

Christians individually and the church collectively ought to respond like the Psalmist:

> Then they cried out to the Lord in their trouble,
> And He saved them out of their distresses.
> He sent His word and healed them,
> And delivered them from their destructions.
> (Psalm 107:19-20).

Embrace the Word of God that makes one wise to salvation.

In Christ there is freedom from the bondage of hypocrisy and lies. Christ alone can save His people from apostasy.

May the grace of God save His people from despising the Bible?

Once a Fertile Church, Now Fruitless

Hosea 9:1-17

Hosea was charged with the responsibility to preach the full counsel of God to the people of God. Preachers today must be sure to preach the full counsel of God exactly the way God gave it to them in His Word.

Apparently the Old Testament church had not heard the full counsel of God because she was consumed with false worship, false doctrine and immoral behavior. The church today suffers the same maladies.

Those introductory remarks show the similarities of the Old Testament church to the New Testament church.

The modern church often avoids the application of these Old Testament messages because they sound so harsh.

For instance, the events in chapter nine describe a church that grieves over God's coming judgment. Today little is said about God's coming judgment on the church.

The desires are pride and power rather than grief and humility.

The Old Testament church had misunderstood the character and nature of God. God's warnings had been plentiful, but generation after generation had ignored God's warnings. Like the church today, they didn't think God meant what He said. God's people must remember that God's promises are not empty threats.

God's judgment may not be immediately demonstrated and therefore not evident in the form of immediate punishment.

Hosea explains this doctrine and issues yet another warning to the Old Testament congregation.
Hosea 9:1

The reference to "other peoples" is an indictment against unbelievers who rejoice in false worship.

False worship may appeal to unconverted sinners, but God is displeased with all false worship (Leviticus 10:1-2).

The Old Testament church committed physical and spiritual adultery by participating in fertility rites on the threshing floor. It was the Old Testament church that continued false worship in the face of God's promise to "punish them for their ways" (Hosea 4:9).

A quick review of a few of God's promises is necessary to bring this into the proper context.

➢ I will avenge the bloodshed of Jezreel on the house of Jehu (Hosea 1:4).

> ➢ I will no longer have mercy on the house of Israel (Hosea 1:6).
> ➢ I will utterly take them away (Hosea 1:6).
> ➢ I will not be your God (Hosea 1:6).
> ➢ I will hedge up your way with thorns (Hosea 2:6).
> ➢ I will destroy her vines and her fig trees (Hosea 2:12).
> ➢ I will make them a forest (Hosea 2:12).
> ➢ I will punish her (Hosea 2:13).
> ➢ I also will reject you from being priest for Me (Hosea 4:6).
> ➢ I also will forget your children (Hosea 4:6).
> ➢ I will change their glory into shame (Hosea 4:7).
> ➢ I will punish them for their ways (Hosea 4:9).
> ➢ I will pour out My wrath on them like water (Hosea 5:10).

How should God's people respond? They should obey God and return to the Lord.

Hosea 6:1

When Hosea uttered this prophecy the northern kingdom enjoyed the prosperity of God's providence. There was plenty of money. The nation as a whole enjoyed great prosperity. About seventy years before the ministry of Hosea, the Bible refers to the ivory house and ten cities built by Ahab during his reign (1 Kings 22:39).

Amos the prophet ministered during the same general period of time as Hosea the prophet. Amos referred to "winter houses, summer houses, houses of ivory, and great houses." These words describe the affluent nature of the Old Testament church (Amos 3:15).

Economic prosperity often creates wealth, but it also creates class divisions among the people. Amos refers to the mistreatment of the poor during these prosperous times.

With the advent of money flowing like water down a stream, comes the prosperity of the church. With plenty of money pouring into the church coffers the church no longer depends on God. Since plenty of people are joining the church new styles of cult worship are necessary to keep people happy.

The worship services are so wonderful! How could God not be happy? The congregation seems to be happy.

The French Revolution introduced a new way of thinking about life. The goal to be a "good man" changed to "a happy man." At the end of the 20th century happiness was not enough. Success and self-fulfillment were necessary for happiness. The happiness of man replaced the quest for the goodness of God.

God's interest is not merely in outward happiness. God is interested in inward goodness.

Since God alone is good, then all goodness must come from God. Loving the goodness of God will result in loving good worship. It is good worship if it is offered to God through the Mediator, the Lord Jesus Christ.

The only way God will be pleased with worship is because of the perfect sacrifice of Jesus Christ.

The sacrifice of Christ brings His people into a right relationship with God by the power of the Holy Spirit. The result is a good relationship, which leads to true worship. If the relationship is right, worship is good. If the relationship is bad, the worship is false.

True worship is always good worship.
False worship appears to be happy worship.

The Lord God almighty tells His congregation, again and again, that false worship is unacceptable.
Hosea 9:4

This is a reference to the hypocrites in the Old Testament church who worship, but it was worship in vain. Their sacrifices did not satisfy God, because they also sacrificed to idols and demons.

The modern church has its share of idols. They have popular preachers, sophisticated theologians, persuasive conference speakers, wonderful singers, the finest buildings and much more. Hypocrisy and idolatry fit together like hand and glove.

Jesus quoted the prophet Isaiah when speaking to the hypocrites during His early ministry (Matthew 15:1-11).

These people draw near to Me with their mouth,

And honor Me with their lips, But their heart is far from Me. And in vain they worship Me, teaching as doctrines the commandments of men.

False teachers were popular during the time of Hosea, but the people rejected the true prophets.
Hosea 9:7

The false prophets set out to flatter the people. False prophets set out to tell the people what the people want to hear.

The church has not always been in such disrepair. There are times when the church is very productive. I'll call it a fertile church.

In fact, Hosea uses an agricultural metaphor to describe the Old Testament Church before it turned away from true worship.

This is the first of four prophetical metaphors spoken by the prophet Hosea to the Old Testament congregation. One is found in this text and the other three are found in chapters ten and eleven.

These four prophetical metaphors were probably announced a couple of years before the fall of the northern kingdom (722 B.C.) because he says, "the days of punishment have come."

I will share this brief illustration to point out the contrast seen in the metaphor about the grapes and the figs. I visited a congregation of God's people and was very familiar with their doctrine and creeds. While I was waiting for the speaker to begin, I picked up a pew Bible and while thumbing through it, I noticed hand written notes in the Book of Daniel. The notes reflected a doctrine and theological system that was precisely opposite of the doctrine of that church. Why was it taught? I don't know, but this I do know; conflicting doctrine that stands in contradiction will always lead to confusion. Confusion may lead to disbelief. God is not a God of confusion or contradiction. After inquiring about those notes the response was a sad but not unusual commentary on the state of the church: "It was once a very faithful church." The grapes and figs represent a once faithful church.

There are many churches that may be able to relate to the title of this chapter: "Once a fertile church, now fruitless."

Now I turn to the metaphor about grapes and figs. Keep in mind that a metaphor is used to draw a comparison between two things.
Hosea 9:10-13

In the first metaphor God compares Himself to someone traveling in a wilderness, literally a desert, and suddenly coming upon a beautiful grape vine loaded with luscious juicy grapes. Grapes found in a barren wilderness would be a delight. It would be like coming upon something you would not expect.

The second metaphor describes the first fruits on the fig

tree in its first season. The Hebrew word *bikkuwrah* translated first fruit refers to the early June fig which ripens on the previous year's sprout and is tender for eating far in advance of the late summer fig. Jeremiah describes the first figs this way: "One basket had very good figs, like the figs that are first ripe" (Jeremiah 24:2).

These metaphors, the grapes and figs, describe God's delight in His children. The prophet demonstrates the relationship God had with his people in the past. When God's people are in the desert of life and there is no place to turn but to the sovereign God who created and sustains them, they bloom into a delightful piece of fruit. God took great delight in His people. They were fruitful like grapes in the wilderness and the first fruits on the fig tree in its first season.

In retrospect the church of every generation ought to remember the words spoken through the mouth of Moses.

> The Lord did not set His love on you nor choose you because you were more in number than any other people, for you were the least of all peoples; but because the Lord loves you, and because He would keep the oath which He swore to your fathers, the Lord has brought you out with a mighty hand, and redeemed you from the house of bondage, from the hand of Pharaoh king of Egypt. Therefore know that the Lord your God, He is God, the faithful God who keeps covenant and mercy for a thousand

generations with those who love Him and keep His commandments; and He repays those who hate Him to their face, to destroy them. He will not be slack with him who hates Him; He will repay him to his face. There you shall keep the commandment, the statutes, the judgments, which I command you today, to observe them. (Deuteronomy 7:7-11)

The Lord loves, chooses, and redeems His people from the bondage of sin and the mark of God's love and grace is evident from the fruit that comes forth.

However, the church did not continue its fruitfulness. The grapes dried up and the figs withered away because of covenant unfaithfulness.

Hosea looks in retrospect and reminds them of their unfaithfulness in times past.
Hosea 9:10

This is a reference to Israel's harlotry in Moab.

> Now Israel remained in Acacia Grove and the people began to commit harlotry with the women of Moab. They invited the people to the sacrifices of their gods, and the people ate and bowed down to their gods. So Israel was joined to Baal of Peor, and the anger of the Lord was aroused against Israel. (Numbers 25:1-3)

Baal was the fertility god in Ancient Near Eastern culture. Although it was alleged that Baal was a fertility god, it did not exist in reality.

Contrary to God's prescription for worship, the Israelite men engaged in sexual rites presumably to gain the favor of the Canaanite gods so their agricultural enterprises would be productive.

It is so easy to trust the sensual realm. You can taste, touch, see, feel, and smell the world around you. It requires a renewed mind, literally a change in the soul, to be able to trust God. Even so, Christians are tempted to gain the favor of those around them rather than the favor of God.

Well begun is not enough.
Hosea 9:15

Gilgal was the pivotal point of return during Israel's conquest and return to the Promised Land. Gilgal was where the covenant of circumcision was renewed. Gilgal was the place where the Old Testament church celebrated the Passover for the first time since they came out of Egypt. Gilgal was the place the congregation assembled to worship their Redeemer.

Gilgal was at one time the picture of the church in its covenant faithfulness and its worship to the true and living God. It was like grapes and figs in the wilderness. Adopting the heathen ways of the surrounding nations, a once fertile church was now fruitless.

Notice what God said about their unfaithfulness. "For

there I hated them." Although the place of worship became a place of corrupt and false worship, the sad truth is that God hated the people who worshipped there.

The Hebrew verb translated into English as *hate* does not mean what contemporary Christians attach to the meaning of the word *hate*. Personal emotions are beside the point when the Bible speaks of God's love or his hatred. Love and hate are not exclusively emotional; there is a rational equity about those words.

Scripture proves that God never turns His back on His church; it is the church that turns away from God and becomes fruitless. When the church turns its back on the Word of God, the result is devastating.

Although individual believers will remain faithful, the church as a whole will feel the effect of a fruitless, sterile life.

So what must God's people do? Return to the Lord both individually and as a church collectively. God's people must be distinctive in doctrine and practice after they return to the Lord.

Yes, return to the Lord, so the Lord will find His church like grapes in the wilderness and like the first fruits on the fig tree in its first season. Pray that she will once again become a fertile church.

The Fruit of Unrighteousness

Hosea 10:1-15

The four prophetical metaphors found in chapters nine through eleven were spoken by Hosea at a critical time in the history of the Old Testament Church.

The first metaphor in chapter nine has two parts, the grapes and the figs, that describe God's delight in His people Israel at a previous time. The church was like grapes and figs in a desert. The fruit was delicious. However, over a period of time the church became sterile and fruitless (Hosea 9:10).

The two metaphors in chapter ten describe the present condition of the Old Testament church just before the fall in 722 B.C. The historical condition of the Old Testament church in the northern kingdom must not overshadow the religious nature of its spiritual depravity.

The Bible describes the church as a miscarrying womb with dry breasts. God spoke through the prophet Hosea and said, "All their wickedness is in Gilgal, For there I hated them"(Hosea 9:15).

There are two dangers for all people, Christians and unbelievers. The first danger is to not worship God and the second danger is to worship Him falsely.

A brief review of God's covenant relationship with his people will put these metaphors in proper perspective. God made a covenant with Adam and Eve, but they broke the covenant. A covenant must either be kept and therefore fulfill its purpose or broken and therefore due punishment may be rendered by the covenant maker.

Around 1000 B.C. God's people were united under the leadership of David and Solomon. God ordained the place and manner of worship at the temple in Jerusalem (1 Chronicles 28:2-19).

When Solomon died the kingdom divided and the northern kingdom under the leadership of Jeroboam established new places to worship; one in the south part of the kingdom at Bethel and one in the north part of the kingdom at Dan. Those places of worship were not ordained by God as the place for His people to assemble and worship. It was the Old Testament equivalent to a New Testament church split (1 Kings 25-33).

Two hundred years later, around 722 B.C., Hosea the prophet observes the religious cult of the Old Testament congregation. He observed the congregation playing the harlot and chasing her lovers (Hosea 2:5-7).

Following God's instruction Hosea warned the people of God's coming judgment, unless they repent and return to the Lord.

The Old Testament church had become a false religious cult because she went after her own lovers, rather than

loving the true and living God.
Hosea 2:13

The modern church emulates the Old Testament church. She loves to follow tradition; she loves the unbiblical and therefore ungodly ways of worship; she loves her own opinion. The Old Testament church had played the harlot for so long she did not know the true and living God.
Hosea 4:1

The modern church says she knows God, but how many of her followers could actually name the Ten Commandments? How many could actually give a clear, concise explanation of who God is in one sentence? In the past, Christians taught their children the doctrine of Scripture from the Children's catechism. One question was: What is God? The answer is: God is a Spirit, infinite, eternal and unchangeable in His being, wisdom, power, holiness, justice, goodness and truth. The church ought to recover that kind of accuracy and theological precision.

False worship and idolatry captivated the Old Testament church and the contemporary church shows evidence of the same problem. There appears to be a close resemblance of the spiritual condition of the church during the time of Hosea to the spiritual condition of the church today.

The two prophetical metaphors in this portion of God's Word paint a vivid picture of the historical as well as the spiritual condition of the church.

In the first metaphor, the Old Testament church is compared to a vine.
Hosea 10:1

The Hebrew text has a verb form (a participle) that is translated *empties* in the New King James Version.

The New International Version translation is "Israel was a spreading vine." The New American Standard Bible translation is "Israel is a luxuriant vine."

You might ask, how can a vine be luxuriant and empty at the same time? Bible scholars offer two possibilities for interpretation.

1. It may be argued that the prophet had in mind a vine with leaves and branches, but little or no fruit.

2. It may refer to a luxurious vine robbed of its fruit by its own disease.

In either case, the Old Testament church failed to produce good fruit because she turned away from the Lord.

This analogy of comparison shows the similarity of the vine to the church and probably for one of the following reasons.

1. A vine has the outward appearance of growth and vigor, but clip the main branch and the vine dies. The question everyone should ask is: Is the main branch spiritual or is it physical and material? If it is spiritual

there must be a source that is eternal. Are you tapped into that eternal source?
Hosea 6:2

2. A vine depends on nutrients to strengthen it and make the foliage appear profuse. The Old Testament church looked for its strength in the wrong place. "My people ask counsel from their wooden idols."
Hosea 4:12

The modern church often patronizes the most recent cultural trend to formulate its worship, mission, and ministry. The principle is the same as asking counsel from wooden idols. Seeking counsel from false gods will provoke God's wrath.
Hosea 5:10

3. A vine requires great care if it is a productive vine. The Old Testament church failed to realize that God was their caretaker. They abused the abundance of God's gifts by offering false worship.
Hosea 2:8

The vast wealth procured by the modern church is from the kind and generous providence of God. Has the modern church been a good steward of God's provision or has she squandered the wealth on false gods? It is a hard question, but it must be answered.

This doctrine is further explained in the metaphor "he brings forth fruit for himself. According to the multitude of his fruit He has increased the altars" (Hosea 10:1).

The "multitude of his fruit" shows how generous God was to His people, but they used His generosity by increasing false worship. God had been good to the Israelites and He had been patient with them, but to abuse the goodness of God was to mock Him.

When God's grace and mercy is in abundance, it seems that the church commits more sins against Him. It seems as if prosperity breeds wickedness.

Therefore the church is referred to as a spreading vine. The church is growing; the church has plenty of programs; the church is full of religious activity.

The vine representing the church puts out its strength in leaves and branches, but produces bad or perhaps no fruit.

The fruit of the Old Testament church was bad because of its rebellious attitude demonstrated by its false worship and irresponsible behavior before God.

God commands His covenant people to singularly love Him, but Hosea reminds them they have broken covenant with God.
Hosea 10:2

A divided heart is always a rebellious heart. Divisions cause so much sin. In Hosea's day the church people were divided over who to worship. Some worship was offered to the living and true God and other worship to the dead and false idols. They loved God, but they loved their idols so much more.

A rebellious heart is subject to swear falsely in making a promise.
Hosea 10:4

It is easy to say empty words. They have no meaning. How many professing Christians say something like this: "I will do such and such or I will not do such and such" but as time passes those words are empty in practice. Perjury does not seem to bother Christians.

Speaking words that are not true will invoke God's wrath, create confusion, and invalidate mutual trusts. It's bad enough that such things happen between Christians, but when they think they can deceive God it is exponentially worse.

The spreading vine of sin will provoke God's wrath.
Hosea 10:10

God warns His people to act quickly by turning to the Lord in faith and repentance. Then they will find out just how much good fruit they may bear.

The words of the Lord Jesus Christ should resonate with every Christian. "I am the vine, you are the branches. He who abides in Me, and I in him, bears much fruit; for without Me you can do nothing" (John 15:5).

The second prophetical metaphor compares the church to a trained heifer.
Hosea 10:11

This metaphor likens the Old Testament Church to a young cow trained to thresh grain. It was a relatively pleasant job walking around the threshing floor until the grain was separated from the stalks. The cow could eat anytime while she was working.

This is compared to the oxen coupled together with yokes and pulling a plough. It would be laborious and difficult to pull the plough.

This metaphor likens the young heifer to the young church full or zeal, excitement, and intensely focused on loving and worshipping God. God demonstrates grace and mercy and the church prospers. As time passes the church losses it zeal and excitement and as the Book of Revelation says, she loses her first love (Revelation 2:4).

How should Christians respond to this doctrine?

Ask yourself these questions. Is the church like a spreading vine that outwardly appears strong and healthy, but inwardly she is spiritually weak and faint? Does she bear little if any fruit?

Is the church like a trained heifer that has forgotten the generous and kind treatment of her master?

Has the church plowed wickedness? Has she eaten the fruit of lies? Has she trusted in her own way?

I would be a malicious prognosticator to try and answer for you as an individual. However as for the church in a general sense, the answer is yes!

The response to all these questions is to seek the Lord. **Hosea 10:12**

It is time to seek the Creator, Redeemer, Governor, and Judge.

There is an immediate and urgent call to seek the Lord in repentance and faith while the Lord may be found.

.

God Loves His Children

Hosea 11:1-11

This is the final of four prophetical metaphors that Hosea used to describe the church. He says the church is like a growing child.

The first metaphor was about the church in retrospect. The next two metaphors was the church in the present time. This last metaphor describes the chronological development of God's relationship with His people. Think of it in terms of watching children grow up and moving from one stage in life to the next.

Since the Bible frequently refers to children in a spiritual sense, we must be careful to discern the father of the children. Some spiritual children have Satan as their father and others are children of God (John 8:44 and 1 John 4:16).

There are those who profess to be children of God, but in reality do not belong to God. There are those who are rebellious children of God who will return to God in due time. Some professing Christians are not actually Christians and some Christians are rebellious.

> For they are not all Israel who are of Israel, nor are they all children because they are the seed of Abraham. . . That is those who are children of the flesh, they are not the children of God; but

the children of the promise are counted as the seed (Romans 9:6-8).

This metaphor describes the child of God who has been rebellious. However, there is hope that the child may repent and receive compassion rather than death. This text begins with the child's past. First, notice how God demonstrates His tender compassion.

Hosea 11:1

This is a lesson of God's love for His children; for those who truly belong to God. If you belong to God, you have to say "God loved me first" (1 John 4:19).

Figuratively speaking, all God's children have been in Egypt at one time or another. The tenderness of this language shows the love of a father for his child. The evidence of His love for His children was bringing them out of Egypt. The Israelites lived in bondage; it was a miserable condition. The Israelites did not do anything to deserve their freedom. However, they were given new life by the grace of God. The sinner lives in bondage to Satan until God's grace gives the sinner new life in Jesus Christ.

How did the children of God respond after God brought them out of Egypt?

Hosea 11:2

The child rebelled against His father by ignoring God's call to repent. His congregation worshipped false gods. They refused God's instruction, even though they cry out "my God, we know You" (Hosea 8:2)!

This familial language of the rebellious child is present throughout the Bible. After God delivered His children to the Promised Land, they still rebelled against Him. Shortly after settling in the good land that God had given them there was talk of false gods.

> And if it seems evil to you to serve the Lord choose for yourselves this day whom you will serve, whether the gods which your fathers served that were on the other side of the River or the gods of the Amorites, in whose land you dwell. But as for me and my house, we will serve the Lord. (Joshua 24:15)

In the Book of Judges, the Old Testament church "chose new gods" (Judges 2:11-12; 10:14).

In the New Testament there is the parable of the rebellious son, mistakenly called the prodigal son (Luke 15:11-32).

God saves his rebellious children by His magnificent grace.

When God looks at His children He remembers how He nurtured them in the past.
Hosea 11:4

God responds to His children with tender care, because His love is unique and perfect, unlike the love expressed by the sinful human race.

This is the second reference to God's love for his children in this chapter. First He said, "when Israel was a child, I loved him" and then God "drew them with bands of love." The Hebrew text leaves some latitude for translating this text into other languages.

The word *drew* in this text comes from a Hebrew word that could be translated *drag*. The word *bands* may be translated *ropes*. Therefore it may be necessary for God to bind His children with a rope and drag them where they need to be. You may apply this to your own life.

God protects, provides and governs His children, (his sheep to use a New Testament simile), but be aware that there are wolves among God's sheep, so says Jesus Christ (Matthew 7:15).

The Apostle Paul warned the Ephesians that savage wolves would come in among them, not sparing the flock (Acts 20:29).

The Galatian church in the New Testament had the problem of rebellion and disbelief. The apostle Paul wrote the Galatians and said, "I marvel that you are turning away so soon from Christ to a different gospel" (Galatians 1:6).

Any frivolous treatment of God's Word represents a turning away from the truth of God to a different gospel. A false gospel based on personal ideas will lead to false worship.

Professing Christians often reject the goodness, kind,

compassionate, merciful, and loving hand of the Lord. It is evident for every period in the history of God's saving grace.
Hosea 11:7

The inclination to turn away from God comes from the sinful nature. The sin nature prefers pride, arrogance, and rebellion instead of humility, respect and obedience.

Even so, God's love is so overwhelming.
Hosea 11:8-9

This is one of those places in the Bible that ungodly men accuse God of being capricious. It is said that God is unchangeable and here, at first glance, it may appear that God changes His mind about punishing the Old Testament church. Obviously that is not true because they were defeated and taken by the enemy into slavery.

God is not like a chameleon so that He changes color to fit the landscape. God is not capricious like humans, changing the mind at the drop of a hat.

God uses human expressions to accommodate Himself to our feeble intelligence when He speaks to us in the Word of God.

The idolatry, immoral behavior, and agnosticism deserved much more punishment. God's love and compassion stirred Him to "not execute the fierceness of My anger."

The Old Testament church left the Father, but the Father did not leave the church. A real child of God will always come back to the Father, even if he or she does rebel. Children of the flesh will continue down the road of rebellion.

A child of God grieves for and hates his sins and turns from them to God more and more as he or she grows up in the Lord. The growing child listens to the Word of God. The growing child agrees with the Word of God and turns to God in faith and practice.

Until His children return to Him, God continues to warn them.

> Hear the Word of the Lord you children of Israel. For the Lord brings a charge against you (Hosea 4:1).
>
> Hear this O priests,
> Take heed O house of Israel
> Give ear O house of the king
> For yours is the judgment
> (Hosea 5:1).
>
> Set the trumpet to your mouth
> Because they have transgressed my covenant
> (Hosea 8:1).
>
> Do not rejoice, O Israel, with joy like other peoples; For you have played the harlot against your God (Hosea 9:1).

These warnings are repeated throughout the Bible and His children will hear His voice.

God's plan is for His children to return to Him in faith and repentance.
Hosea 11:10-11

Jesus said, "I go to prepare a place for you" and the Lord speaking through the mouth of Hosea said, "I will let them dwell in their houses."

God's growing children will return to the Lord and they will walk after the Lord.

The great joy for Christians is to dwell with the Lord forever.

Biblical Repentance

Hosea 11:12 - 12:14

Despite what many contemporary preachers may say, the bulk of the Bible warns its readers of God's coming judgment.

The book of Hosea reveals the heart of God and His character. He is patient and longsuffering. God demonstrates His love for His sinful people by warning them of the consequences of sin.

Hosea's message is a historical account of the Old Testament church just before it fell into a state of religious *dyslogia*.

Dyslogia describes a condition of pathological confusion. It is a condition that prevents a person from expressing intelligent discourse because of faulty reasoning or speech, due to a mental disorder. The Old Testament Church was in a state of religious *dyslogia*. They were unable to worship God in a manner acceptable to God. They worshipped, but it was false worship.

Hosea described the state of the church with four prophetical metaphors: The grapes and figs, the spreading vine, the trained heifer and growing child. These figures of speech reflect God's love for and delight in His children, but also His anger and disapproval. It is faulty reasoning to dismiss this whole scene and God's warning, alleging or should I say hoping this prophecy was for other people at other times.

The people thought Hosea's prophecy was for someone else. Maybe Hosea's message was for the person sitting next to them in the worship service. Maybe the Old Testament Church thought their prosperity and religious cult worship would save them.

The New Testament Church, in its youth, thought the same thing. "I am rich, have become wealthy, and have need of nothing" (Revelation 3:17).

Hosea describes, with picturesque language, the Old Testament church and Israel as a body politic.
Hosea 11:12 and 12:1

The tone of Hosea's message is loud and clear. His people surround Him with lies. Their lies increase each day.

The sinless human race came face to face with the charming liar named Satan. Adam and Eve believed Satan and now "The wicked are estranged from the womb; They go astray as soon as they are born, speaking lies" (Psalm 58:3).

God preserves a remnant that "speak no lies" and they offer true worship to the true and living God (Zephaniah 3:13).

Lies are not real, they are illusions. It is always dangerous to trust illusions. Some of the most scathing remarks that came out of the mouth of the Lord Jesus Christ were against liars (John 8:42-47).

Paul warned the church that the time would come when some will speak "lies in hypocrisy" (1 Timothy 4:1-3).

Hosea has already explained that Ephraim, representing Israel, had "joined to idols" (Hosea 4:17).

One of the most heinous sins associated with idolatry is to speak lies to God in worship.

Idolatry is false worship and anything false is a lie. Obviously the Old Testament church had postured itself against God by their exponential engagement in false worship. The church surrounded God with lies.

I use the word exponential because God said His people "daily increases lies." It seems as if the people were devising new lies every day.

The consequences are terrible. The lies will actually increase the ruin of the church. The congregation, alleged worshippers, conjured up lies by their own imaginations.

The New Testament Church is no different than the Old Testament church. During its infancy, the Lord Jesus Christ testified about the condition of the church. "You do not know that you are wretched, miserable, poor, blind, and naked" (Revelation 3:17).

The lies and deceit lead to religious dyslogia. The Apostle Paul said, "even as they did not like to retain God in their knowledge, God gave them over to a debased mind. . ." (Romans 1:28ff).

Although Hosea's prophecy is to the northern kingdom the progeny of the church may experience God's judgment.
Hosea 12:2

The northern kingdom and eventually the southern kingdom would not escape God's judgment. The New Testament church also faces the possibly of God's judgment coming upon them.

> For we must all appear before the judgment seat of Christ, that each one may receive the things done in the body, according to what he has done, whether good and bad. (2 Corinthians 5:10)

God's warnings apply to every generation of God's people.

The way to avoid God's judgment is biblical repentance. Christians talk about repentance, but do Christians really understand its doctrine and meaning? The only way repentance can be understood is by the Word of God.

The prophet Zechariah called the Old Testament congregation to repentance. This occasion is after the seventy year exile and the return of the exiles to

Jerusalem (520 B.C). You would think the Old Testament church would be humbled by God's hand of judgment after a seventy year exile, but God immediately warns them to repent. Read this text carefully in its historical context to grasp the impact of this occasion (Zechariah 1:1-6).

Repentance is about returning to the Lord. Repentance ought to be part of the spiritual exercise every day, because sinful people are apt to turn away from the Lord.

The New Testament use of the word repentance sheds a bit more light on the doctrine of repentance. The Greek word often translated repentance literally means "a change of mind."

A change of mind will ultimately mean a change in direction. For example, if you are convinced in your mind that walking into a den of rattlesnakes is safe, then without a change of mind, you will walk to your death.

Biblical repentance means the sinner understands the sin in his or her life and with a change of mind endeavors to turn away from sin and returns to the Lord. Just as Christians pray for so many things, they should pray for the grace of repentance.

I hope the Word of God through the mouth of Hosea will speak to you about biblical repentance, because God Himself has spoken.
Hosea 12:10

The application of this verse is very simple. Preachers must preach the full of counsel of God and the congregation must listen to the full counsel of God. One very important doctrine in the Word of God is repentance.

The concept of biblical repentance is abundant throughout the book of Hosea. Pay attention to God!
Hosea 12:6

The English word *return* in the Hebrew text is an imperfect verb which indicates an incomplete action or either removed from reality as potential action.

Most translators take the action of the verb *return* to be potential in the form of a command.

The potentiality of God's people returning to Him has inspired historical evidence in the life of Jacob. Jacob called all who were with him to put away foreign gods and return to Bethel, which means House of God (Genesis 35:9-15).

Why is the call to repentance a recurring message throughout the Bible especially in the book of Hosea? God calls His people to repentance over and over because He is patient and longsuffering.

God knows the condition of a sinful heart. He knows the sin nature that dwells within you. No one is exempt from the sin nature, which produces sinful thoughts and acts. The Apostle Paul said, "For the good that I will to do, I do not do; but the evil I will not to do that I practice" (Romans 7:19).

The biblical evidence and the experience of life reveal the need for repentance. A saved sinner will experience the shame for sinning against God. It is then that a sinner will be able to return to the Lord and plead for grace and mercy.

Repentance and worship are inseparably connected. About one hundred years after the prophecy of Hosea the prophet Jeremiah preached to the church in the southern kingdom about repentance. Jeremiah's message from God was, "If you repent, I will restore you, that you may worship me" (Jeremiah 15:19).

Repentance and worship are inseparable. God will find your worship acceptable if you repent and return to Him.

Sometimes Christians use the word repentance as a synonym for conversion, which easily provokes confusion. Conversion is the occasion of the Holy Spirit giving the sinner a new heart and a renewed mind to believe God's saving grace. A new heart must precede repentance. God must change the disposition of the heart so as to enable one to believe and repent.

The call to repentance is universal. In Paul's sermon to the Athenians he said, "Truly, these times of ignorance God overlooked, but now commands all men everywhere to repent" (Acts 17:30).

If you have not been born again by the Spirit of God, ask God to have mercy on your soul and give you new life in Christ so you will be able to repent. If you have been born again by the Spirit of God, Christ commands you to repent.

There may be someone thinking privately, "but there is some sin in my life that I can't overcome." Perhaps that is true, because it has become a habit and is hard to break, but the child of God will begin by confessing the sin.

When the mind changes and the sin becomes a hated sin, the inclination to sin will be suppressed, and the sinner will endeavor to repent, let me repeat - endeavor to repent.

Someone will probably ask, "will repentance save the church from the judgment of God?" Repentance is evidence of a saved church, but repentance will not necessarily save the church from God's judgment.

Obviously Hosea does not mean that the Old Testament church and Israel as a body politic would be spared destruction as a whole. Thousands of these Old Testament saints were killed in the wars that preceded the final siege against them in 722 B.C. But a remnant did survive and they found themselves in captivity. The promise of restoration is to those who repent and return to the Lord.

Today, as in Hosea's day, the church is in a state of confusion and disorder. There is an abundance of pride, lust, and covetousness. There is a self-righteous spirit leading to a worldly secularism and a disregard for the soul and eternity.

All of that would be resolved if the church would consider biblical repentance!

God calls *us,* the whole church, to "Come, let us return to the Lord" (Hosea 6:1).

More specifically God calls the individual "So you, by the help of your God, Return" (Hosea 12:6).

The clearest expression of a prophets pleading to repent comes from the prophet Joel.

> Now therefore says the Lord, Turn to Me with all your heart, with fasting, with weeping, and with mourning. So rend your heart, and not your garments; Return to the Lord your God For He is gracious and merciful, Slow to anger and of great kindness. . .(Joel 2:12-13).

Did You Forget God?

Hosea 13:1-16

The symbolism that God used to describe His relationship to the Old Testament church during the life of Hosea is that of a divine divorce. The church committed adultery against God by their false worship. They went through the motions for worship, but it was false worship. God would not tolerate false worship, so he divorced his adulteress church.

The motivation behind Hosea's prophecy was to warn the Old Testament of the coming judgment. To keep this in perspective the ultimate final judgment is Hell.

The passion of Hosea's prophecy was a plea for repentance. The saving grace of God ultimately leads to repentance and the promise of Heaven.

Hosea issued one warning after the other during his forty year ministry. We come to the end of the prophecy and you might wonder if God has anything different to say. Yes, God has something different to say, something you may not want to hear, but something different.

Hosea's prophecy refers to Ephraim as the representative for Israel and Israel represents the Old Testament church. The prophet placed Ephraim equal to

Israel; therefore Ephraim was the church in a collective sense in that context.

The shift in the use of the word Ephraim in verse one reflects a change from speaking to the whole church to the individual in the church.
Hosea 13:1

Now the prophet speaks of Ephraim as an individual among the tribes of Israel. Ephraim is one among the many. With a couple of exceptions, God has spoken through Hosea warning the church collectively of its rebellion and sin. Now God moves to the individual in the church who rebels against God.

The idea of individual sin reminds me of a cartoon where an old preacher said to the congregation, "The sermon this morning is about sin. I've been here for about twenty five years and I could be more specific."

The message from the old preacher comes across loud and clear, because God alone can illumine you and convict you of your rebellion and sins.

Ephraim's sin and rebellion which was continual finally brought about its own destruction.
Hosea 13:2

After they worshipped Baal, it was so palatable they coveted more idols and their false worship grew worse and worse. Satan is charming! He makes false worship feel good.

Did You Forget God?

Self-destruction is the natural course for an unrepentant sinner.

The individual unrepentant sinner progressively moves from bad to worse until he eventually forgets God.

When an individual forgets God there will be an effect on the whole church.

If the individual sinner in the church forgets the Lord, it will always affect the witness of the church.

God warns His people over and over again in Scripture not to forget Him, but the church has time and again forgotten the Lord. The church, excited by her own agenda, gradually forgets her first love.

You may read for yourself and trace the history of how God's people forget him (Deuteronomy 8:11-17).

God remembered His people, but nearly one hundred years later the Old Testament church forgot the Lord their God, and served the Baals in false worship (Judges 3:7).

Christians don't just forget about God overnight. It takes time and effort to forget God. Even with God's blessing, they still forgot God.
Hosea 13:5-6

Notice the progressive steps in their apostasy.

"I knew you in the wilderness" reveals the intimate

relationship between God and his people in the beginning. See Jeremiah 2:1-6 to read about God's unique relationship with His people.

"In the land of great drought" reminded the church that they were destitute in the desert and turned to God in faith and repentance.

"When they had pasture, they were filled" is evidence of how God furnished an abundance in the Promised Land.

"They were filled and their heart was exalted." The more God provided material wealth, the more they praised their own efforts. Rather than humility in worship, it was arrogance in rebellion.

Finally they forgot God altogether.

They focused on their worldly possessions. It is the pride of men to say "I have become rich." Look at what I am worth, I, I, I (Hosea 12:8).

They focused on their accomplishments. God warned His people about this while they sojourned in the wilderness. God said, "when your heart is lifted up and you forget the Lord your God then say in your heart, my power and the might of my hand have gained me this wealth" (Deuteronomy 8:11-18).

They focused on their self-importance (Isaiah 47:8).

The individual unrepentant sinner progressively moves

from bad to worse until he eventually forgets God.
Hosea 13:2

"Now they sin more and more."

The Hebrew word translated *more and more* literally means *to add*.

It means they continued in their sin, increased their sin and intensified their sin.

> ➤ They adopted false religious practices.

> ➤ They continued in false religious practices after being warned.

> ➤ They increased in false religious practices.

> ➤ They intensified their false religious practices.

> ➤ Every little act of sin tends to increase the next sin.

> ➤ Every little sin against the conscience hardens the conscience.

> ➤ Soon sin becomes a comfortable friend.

> ➤ Finally sin is fully embraced and God is forgotten.

The prophet Hosea says they sinned more and more according to their skill. They increased in their sins as they increased in their understanding of false gods. The general principle of accountability is the fundamental concept.

They "Made for themselves molded images." They did it for <u>themselves</u>, not for God.

If the image was self-made, then it was under self-control.

What happens when someone forgets God and continues the slippery slope of sin?
Hosea 13:3

They will be like the morning cloud which has no substance and disappears without any notice.

They will be like the early dew that passes away. It sparkles for an hour, and then it soon disappears.

They are like chaff blown off from a threshing floor which is worthless.

They are like smoke from a chimney that accomplishes nothing.

Hosea's message from God is manifestly clear. God's judgment is upon those who forget the Lord.
Hosea 13:9

Destruction seemed imminent for the Old Testament church. However, God preserved the Old Testament church even through all their foolish prideful arrogant wanderings. Now God is about to withdraw his grace and mercy only because they had forgotten their God.

These questions should be on every heart and mind of every professing Christian. Where am I as an individual? Where is our church collectively? What will the Lord do?

If individuals forget the Lord, then the church collectively will eventually forget the Lord.

There is hope for the child of God because God never forgets His children.

God calls His children to return to Him. They would be wise to remember that God alone can "ransom them from the power of the grave [and] redeem them from death" (Hosea 14:13).

If anyone asks, "did you forget God?" I hope you will be able to say no! "My hope is in Jesus Christ, so I say thanks be to God who gave me the victory through the Lord Jesus Christ."

The Telos of Words

Hosea 14:1-9

The Old Testament church was much like the church of our time. She was full of pride and overflowing with wealth. The assets of Christian churches in the world today run into the billions of dollars. I'm sure you may think of just a few churches whose combined assets are over one hundred million dollars and that doesn't include the cash flow.

Even though the Old Testament church, like the New Testament church, was full of pride and overflowing with wealth, the prophet preached against the problem of secularism. The church then as now drank too deeply in the gods of the age.

Secularism is one of those gods. Secularism is the world view that supplies the resources for believers and unbelievers to develop false gods. Secularism is charming, but deceitful.

God's displeasure with the Old Testament Church was expressed through the symbolic experiences of marriage and divorce.

The symbolical divorce was not for the purpose of escaping a bad marriage, but a punishment to awaken the church to her senses.

The relationship between God and His bride was severed because God's bride, the church, went after other lovers. It was false hope.

Sinners tend to entertain false hope because they are "bent on backsliding" from God (Hosea 11:7).

Even though sinners are disinclined to remain faithful, God is inclined to "heal their backsliding."
Hosea 14:4

The child of God may be healed only by God's saving grace. The ultimate healing comes because the Lord Jesus Christ propitiates the wrath of God. Christ came "to make propitiation for the sins of the people" (Hebrews 2:17).

Christians should understand the meaning and use of the word *propitiate* for two reasons. First, it is used in the Word of God. Anytime God uses a word it should not be foreign to His children. Secondly, it is the word that defines the healing of a sinful soul. Propitiation is the satisfaction of God's wrath. It was the sacrifice of Christ that propitiated God's wrath against the sinner.

Propitiation is the condition necessary for God's people to be healed of their backsliding.

The Old Testament church faced the possibility of judgment because she had departed from the Word of God as the ruling principle in faith and life.

However, the church will always have a remnant. Some

will always be faithful, but many will be unfaithful like Gomer was to Hosea.

The true child of God will always return.
Hosea 14:7

God instructs His children to "return to the Lord." No matter how far you move away from the Lord, these words will ring in your ears: "return to the Lord."

Every day you hear words, maybe even 1000's of words. Some of those words are important and some are not. Some people just talk until they think of something to say. Although some people may use an abundance of useless words, some words may be important, in fact, very important.

The title of this chapter is "The Telos of Words." The words in this title are important. The word *telos* is a Greek noun which means that something is brought to perfection. *Telos* refers to fulfillment.

When Jesus was about to breathe his last breath on the cross He said, "It is finished." His sacrificial work on earth was complete and perfect. He fulfilled His purpose on earth. The Greek word for "it is finished" is a verb derived from the noun *telos*.

The word *telos* is associated with purpose. Everything you do has a purpose and if there is purpose there must be an end goal.

The purpose of Hosea's words will have eternal

consequences. His words warn God's people of the coming judgment. His words also give them hope by calling them to return to the Lord.

In his final message Hosea told the people to "return to the Lord with words."
Hosea 14:1-2

God admonished the Old Testament church to bring words with them when they return to worship the Lord. This put an end to the notion that God would be satisfied with their sacrifices. The sacrifice itself was not sinful. However, the sacrifices were repugnant to God. The people offered sacrifices without mercy and the knowledge of God (Hosea 6:6).

They were proud of their own power and ability. They trusted Baal rather than the Lord for salvation. They trusted their own strength, their false superstitions, and their man-made religious schemes.

The Lord wanted them to bring words because they had been worshipping the Lord in their own wisdom. Their false confidence had blinded them. They thought they had all the right answers without consulting the Word of God.

They offered worship, but it was false worship. They sang songs, but didn't pay attention to the words. I hope you pay attention to the words when you sing, because God is only interested in the words being truthful and coming from a right heart.

The Telos of Words

Every individual in the Old Testament congregation was in a covenant relationship with God. Their knowledge of God was obscure and maybe even contrary to the nature and character of God. They recited their vows, but they didn't have a clue what they meant.

The Lord does not want you to say empty words in worship! The Lord repudiates empty words on any occasion, especially if you offer them in worship.

Many of the people in the Old Testament church found the doctrine in the Word of God repulsive to their ears. Likewise many people find the words of Jesus Christ offensive.

The words that come from God will have eternal worth, but "for every idle word men may speak, they will give account of it in the day of judgment" (Matthew 12:36).

The universal call to every professing believer and to every congregation on the earth is "return to the Lord with words" that are acceptable to the God of heaven and earth.

Those words must come from a redeemed heart, expressed by personal feelings for the Redeemer. The words must correspond with the words found in Holy Scripture.

God will accept your worship when you take His words with you and return to the Him.

Return to the Lord

> ➤ Bring acceptable words of humble confession.

> ➤ Bring words of forgiveness.

> ➤ Bring words of petition.

> ➤ Bring words from a repentant and thankful heart.

If you are a child of the true and living God, you are liberated from pride and arrogance.

> Let no one cheat you of your reward, taking delight in false humility...and intruding into those things which he has not seen, vainly puffed up by his fleshly mind (Colossians 2:18).

If anyone is vainly puffed up by his fleshly mind then he is in rebellion against God. God will not accept words from the proud heart.

God has questions that every individual must answer.
Hosea 14:9

Who is wise? Let him understand these things. There is no explanation given for these things. He must mean these words, which God had given to them through the mouth of Hosea.

Who is prudent? The word prudent comes from a Hebrew word that basically refers to discernment. Sometimes it is translated into English as intelligent and understanding. An intelligent discerning person with understanding will know *them*. There is no explicit explanation for *them* but in this context it must mean the words they heard from God.

God gave His children words so they might understand His nature and character and their sinful estate.

Words are necessary to understand the holiness of God. If you do not contemplate God's infinite transcendence, you will never experience His immanent love.

Words are necessary to understand the sinfulness of the human race. To know that your sin is contrary to God's holiness and that the two shall never meet is to know the need of reconciliation, forgiveness, and the promise of an eternal favorable relationship with your holy God.

The words of knowledge and wisdom call everyone everywhere to "believe on the Lord Jesus Christ and you will be saved" (Acts 16:31).

If the Holy Spirit has given you a new heart and wrapped you in the righteousness of Jesus Christ then you will trust Christ alone for a favorable eternal relationship with the Lord God almighty.

Then you will have wisdom, understanding, prudence, and knowledge. Then you will always return to the Lord with words of humble confession, forgiveness, petition, repentance, and thanksgiving.

About the Author

Martin Murphy has a B.A. in Bible from Columbia International University and Master of Divinity from Reformed Theological Seminary. Martin spent nearly thirty years in the class room, the pulpit, the lectern, the study, and the library. He now devotes most of his time consolidating academic and practical gains by writing books. He and his wife Mary live in Dothan, Alabama. He is the author of fourteen Christian books.

The Church: First Thirty Years, 344 pages, ISBN 9780985618179, $15.95. This book is an exposition of the Book of Acts. It will help Christians understand the purpose, mission, and ministry of the church.

The Dominant Culture: Living in the Promised Land, 172 pages, ISBN 970991481118, $11.95. This book examines the culture of Israel during the period of the Judges. It explains how worldviews influence the church and it reveals biblical principles to help Christians learn how to live in the culture.

My Christian Apology, 98 pages, ISBN 9780984570874, $7.95. This book investigates the doctrine of Christian apologetics. It explains rational Christian apologetics.

The Essence of Christian Doctrine, 200 pages, ISBN 9780984570812, $12.95. This book was written so that pastors and laymen would have a quick reference to major biblical doctrines. Dr. Steve Brown says it was written, "with clarity and power about the verities of the Christian faith and in a way that makes a difference in how we live."

Theological Terms in Layman Language, 130 pages, ISBN 9780985618155, $8.95. This book was written so that simple words like faith or not so simple words like aseity are explained in plain language. Theological Terms in Layman Language is easy to read and designed for people who want a brief definition for theological terms. The terms are in layman friendly language.

Brief Study of the Ten Commandments, 164 pages, ISBN 9780991481163, $10.95. This book will help Christians discover or re-discover the meaning of the Ten Commandments.

The Present Truth, 164 pages, ISBN 9780983244172, $8.95. Each chapter examines a topic relative to the Christian life. Topics such as church, sin, anger, marriage, education and more.

Doctrine of Sound Words: Summary of Christian Theology, 423 pages, ISBN 9780991481125, $16.95. This is a book of Christian doctrine in topical format. It covers a wide range of theological topics such as, the triune God, creation, providence, sin, justification, repentance, Christian liberty, free will, marriage and divorce, Christian fellowship, et al). There are thirty three topics beginning with 'Holy Scriptures' and ending with 'The Last Judgment.' It is a systematic theology for laymen based on the full counsel of God.

Friendship: The Joy of Relationships, ISBN 9780986405518, 48 pages, $6.49. This is the kind of book that friends give each other and share the principles with each other. If friends do not feel comfortable sharing these relationship principles with each other, the friendship may not really exist. Friendship involves a relationship of distinction. It is a relationship that respects the dignity of another person. The Bible teaches a different version of what it means to be a friend than the popular culture teaches. There are many occasions when friends say they are friends, but they are not friends. 'Even my own familiar friend in whom I trusted, who ate my bread, has lifted up his heel against me' (Psalm 41:9). A true friend will endure and sacrifice for a friend. 'A friend loves at all times' (Proverbs 17:7) and 'there is a friend who sticks closer than a brother' (Proverbs 18:24).

Ultimate Authority for the Soul, ISBN 9780986405501, 151 pages, $9.99. What is the ultimate authority for human beings? This book examines that question and concludes that every rational being has some recognition of God as the ultimate authority. Although God is the ultimate authority, He confers His authority by means of the Word of God. The author examines Psalm 119 to build a defense for the ultimate authority for the soul. Although this book was written for Christians, the author builds the case that authority is a principle necessary to maintain sanity and order in the family, the church and civil society. The Word of God connects the soul with reality.

Constitutional Authority in a Postmodern Culture, ISBN 9780985618124, 56 pages, $5.95. This book shows the validity of constitutional authority and the invasion of postmodern theories in western culture. Postmodern theory has assaulted the western culture on the battleground of absolute truth and reality. Postmodern theory places human experience over abstract objective principles. Christians have a constitution known as the Bible so they will know the truth of reality. The last chapter is devoted to cultural reformation.

Learn to Pray: Biblical Doctrine of Prayer, ISBN 9780986405563, 107 pages, $7.95. This book examines the Lord's model prayer so Christians may learn to pray according to the Lord's instruction. It also reviews some of the prayers of the apostle Paul to discover his doctrine of prayer. Pastor James Perry wrote the Foreword with insight and experience. "I am impressed with this book on the subject of Learn to Pray. It is stated briefly and succinctly following the model and example of the Lord's Prayer. There is considerable practical instruction on the meaning and implication about purposeful and biblical prayer and it will serve as a useful primer for all who apply the prayer principles. The reader will doubtlessly return to the instruction frequently for the practical help it offers."

The god of the Church Growth Movement, 95 pages
ISBN 9780986405587, $6.95.   This work includes a
brief explanation of modernity and its effect on church
growth. It is a critical analysis of the church growth
movement found in every branch of the Protestant
church.